ANEW

Complete Shorter Poetry

Also by Louis Zukofsky
from New Directions

"A"

ANEW

Complete Shorter Poetry

LOUIS ZUKOFSKY

With a foreword by
ROBERT CREELEY

A NEW DIRECTIONS BOOK

Stanza breaks are not indicated after the last lines on the following pages:
9–18, 21, 23, 34, 41, 49, 57, 65, 82, 84–85, 88, 92, 111–12, 115, 121, 123–24, 127,
130, 134, 135–37, 144, 151, 162, 166, 212, 231, 246–52, 254–57, 260, 262–65,
270, 274, 281–93, 295, 297–300, 302–4, 308, 312–13, 316.
All other page breaks coincide with the end of a stanza or a poem.

Manufactured in the United States of America
New Directions Books are printed on acid-free paper
First published by The John Hopkins University Press in 1997
and as a New Directions Paperbook (NDP1192) in 2011
Published simultaneously in Canada by Penguin Books Canada Limited

Library of Congress Cataloging-in-Publication Data
Zukofsky, Louis, 1904–1978.
[Poems. Selections]
Anew: complete shorter poetry / Louis Zukofsky;
with a foreword by Robert Creeley.
p. cm.—(New Directions paperbook; NDP1192)
Previously published: Complete short poetry.
Baltimore: Johns Hopkins University Press, c1991.
Includes index.
ISBN 978-0-8112-1872-6 (paperbook: acid-free paper)
I. Title.
PS3549.U47A6 2011
811'.52—dc22   2010021430

10 9 8 7 6 5 4 3 2

New Directions Books are published for James Laughlin
by New Directions Publishing Corporation
80 Eighth Avenue, New York, NY 10011

Contents

Foreword

The measure of Louis Zukofsky's complex and incomparable poems will be finally the one he himself has provided in his preface to *A Test of Poetry* (1948): "The test of poetry is the range of pleasure it affords as sight, sound, and intellection. This is its purpose as art." To that one may add another quotation from a crucial essay in *Prepositions* (1967), "Poetry, / *For My Son When He Can Read*," written in 1946:

> How much what is sounded by words has to do with what is seen by them—and how much what is at once sounded and seen by them crosscuts an interplay among themselves—will naturally sustain the scientific definition of poetry we are looking for. To endure it would be compelled to integrate these functions: time, and what is seen in time (as held by a song), and an action whose words are actors of or, if you will, mimes composing steps as of a dance that at proper instants calls in the vocal cords to transform it into plain speech.

The poet's "major aim," as he says in this essay, "is not to show himself but that order that of itself will speak to all men."

"Order," then, is the defining prospect of all Zukofsky's work, but it is an order peculiarly without threat or implicit dogma. One can now recognize his situation as being, finally, far more an example of the encroaching dilemmas of Modernism than his elders, Pound, Eliot, or Joyce, who had offered its initial definitions, could either recognize or anticipate. In fact, Zukofsky is impeccably placed to be the consummate person of the period in every respect. Born in New York's Lower East Side in 1904—the year Henry James returned to visit, as Zukofsky liked to remind one—he was the brilliant son of Russian immigrant parents, neither of

vii

whom spoke English, and he completed an M.A. at Columbia at age twenty. What engaged him centered in history and politics, what a people have been and might be, and what factors are critical to either an understanding or a practice relating. So both Henry Adams and Marx are crucial to his thinking, and as a poet his thought again and again returns to the crisis of how a world shall manage coherence, given the chaos and dereliction of its formal means.

One does well to recall even some general sense of the time, with its increasing industrialization, immigration, urban growth, political ferment and shift, a major war, a boom economy and subsequent bust, a rejection of much that the past had seemed to qualify and secure, and, most of all, a rush to the new, a secularization and flattening "humanism," and a culminating depression as approach to the "Second World War." The perceptive critic Bruce Comens proposes a reading of the period's literature using "strategy" and "tactics" for context, thus to recognize that Pound, for one, moves *strategically*, presumes an authority enabling him, whereas Zukofsky, and the Williams of *Paterson*, are committed to *tactics*, to response and improvisation, and their prosody in either case is expectably far more various in its resources despite the fact that either would consider Pound, as did Eliot, "il miglior fabbro." In fact, it is not simply that Pound was "the better craftsman" but that his initiating materials permitted such a stable target for his practice. The Pound of the *Pisan Cantos* is a very different poet indeed than the one who began this great work.

Fitting enough that one of the first poems here should be such an amalgam of technique so echoing the various habits of Pound, Eliot, and Joyce, with a collage of quoted materials, an opaque diversity of sources and worked-for difficulties, but also with a tone altogether Zukofsky's—who hears far more intimately the accumulating past, as in lines 54 to 60, or as here holds to the complexly human:

238 If horses could but sing Bach, mother,—
239 Remember how I wished it once—
240 Now I kiss you who could never sing Bach,
         never read Shakespeare.

Pound's acceptance of "Poem beginning 'The'" for *The Ex-
ile* in a letter dated August 18, 1927, began a critical relation-
ship with Zukofsky, just that Pound was a defining measure
of the possibilities of the art. Even more useful was Pound's
response to the opening sections of Zukofsky's long poem
"*A*," which he had begun, as he notes to Pound in a letter
December 12, 1930, before he had opportunity to see the
emerging form of the *Cantos:*

> As for the history of the matter: when I started the
> thing late 1927 or early 1928, I had not seen the 3 Mts.
> edtns. of your Cantos. Had read only the early ones in
> *Lustra* & 4, 5 & 6 in *Poems 1918–21. . . . "The"* was a
> direct reply to *The Waste Land*—meant to avoid T.S.E's
> technique, line etc (tho I see how much more lucid it is
> than my own) occasional slickness, but intended to tell
> him why, spiritually speaking, a wimpus was still possi-
> ble and might even bear fruit of another generation.
> Didn't like his Wagnerian leit motives, so *I* ended, or
> so I think, by doing something more discursive, more a
> matter of sequential statement—*Pope* maybe in modern
> dress, but the positive getting the better of the satire in
> opening First Movement, parts of two and most of 5
> and 6. But on the whole, left merely with the *promise* of
> the last lines *trans* from Yehoash—"shall be."
> "*A*"'s intention was to make that *promise good.*

He continues, "When 'The' came out, the charge by ⟨of⟩
those who 'are supposed to know' was *Wasteland*. I didn't
think so—Bill [Williams] said *no*, you implied (?) no (?) by
printing it in Exile 3, Taupin with a foreign ear has said no.'"

This "charge" of "influence" was characteristic of a per-
sistent misapprehension that could only read Zukofsky and
other of the Objectivists—George Oppen and Charles Rez-
nikoff among them—as an effect or consequence of such
previous authority. In retrospect, one may well agree with
the judgment Steven Helming offers in this compact sum-
mary: "No poet is in touch at so many points with so much
of the world around him; no poet has written so comprehen-
sively of domestic life; and no poet has undertaken so sus-
tained and original an effort to make political poetry possi-
ble in this century of poetic and political extremes."

Most striking is the grounding of Zukofsky's terms, their substantial reference, and always their singular wit. His resources are the quickness and range of his intelligence and his unique hearing of phonic patterns, which makes them far more than metaphoric or analogous in his work. The pace and sounding in #5 (*"Ferry"*) of "29 Poems" is active instance:

> Gleams, a green lamp
> In the fog:
> Murmur, in almost
> A dialogue . . .

These early poems, with their emphasized if ironically muted political and intellectual detail, are conscious of both their authority and ambition and the company they would hope to keep. But the innate power is immediately evident, in the character of the intelligence and in the quiet genius of the prosody. " *'Mantis,'* " with its complement, " *'Mantis,' An Interpretation,"* manages to use the sestina with all its complicating metrical demands to make vivid the condition of the poor of that harsh time, the Depression, so that, in the setting of a New York subway, this utterly unexpected and defenseless insect becomes their manifest at the close:

> Fly, mantis, on the poor, arise like leaves
> The armies of the poor, strength: stone on stone
> And build the new world in your eyes, Save it!

In the commentary *"An Interpretation,"* Zukofsky spells out the complex ground of his thinking and the facts addressed, to come to this definition of what he has hoped to compose: ". . . the simultaneous, / The diaphanous, historical / In one head."

Whatever the effect of Objectivism as a literary movement, its company was intensive and significant, and the poets so made public are, as the Imagists before them, both served and diminished by such title. In retrospect, the occasion seems a political contrivance sponsored by Pound with Harriet Monroe's agreement: "Wonners will nevuнн cease. I have just recd. nooz from Harriet that she is puttin you at the wheel for the Spring cruise [Oct. 24, 1930]." The issue of *Poetry* in question was published February 1931 with Zukofsky's article, "Sincerity and Objectification," and poems by those now known as the Objectivists—George Oppen, Carl Rakosi, Charles Reznikoff, and Zukofsky himself. There were also contributions from W. C. Williams, Robert McAlmon, Basil Bunting, and Kenneth Rexroth. Only Lorine Niedecker seems missing, but it would not be until 1946 that her first collection, *New Goose*, appeared, and then there would be almost twenty more years till her second book, *My Friend Tree*, was published by the Scots poet and artist, Ian Hamilton Finlay.

Such digression may be questioned and yet it makes clear a situation Zukofsky both knew and dealt with as the place of his own art. The poem *"Barely* and *widely,"* which is *envoi* to an initial book of that title published in 1958 by Celia Zukofsky, is very effective evidence of how closely this world of father, mother, and son did hold, and how articulately its love served them. The collection *Anew* sounds throughout the range of these bonding, locating relations, the pervasive, engendering thought, and the sounds that echo through all, puns become paean. There is so much in this respect to emphasize that one must offer the evocative simplicity and clarity of "4 Other Countries" for all else one might well say: "paradise\our\speech."

One recalls that, for Zukofsky, "Objective" is far more than a literary term or even, in usual sense, a philosophic one. In the sixth movement of *"A"*—he quotes the lines in the third section of his essay for the Objectivist issue of *Poetry*—he makes emphatic the recurring point: "An objective—nature as creator—desire for what is objectively perfect, / Inextricably the direction historic and contemporary particulars"—which, in the essay, he expands to further qualifications, among them, "The desire for an inclusive object." The parallel with music is very clear. That way of *saying something*—"wherein the ideas present themselves sensuously and intelligently and are of no predatory intention"—delighted him as that subtlety of sounding mind, so making order an experienced form, an issue of physical body. The poetry is always a premise of sounds, as he notes in his extraordinary poem celebrating W. C. Williams, "Songs of Degrees," #5: "But to / the expanse / of his / *mind* // who heard / that word / before."

The Catullus translations are an instruction in every respect, just that translation was such an intimate and determining value for Zukofsky, meaning what it says it does, *to carry over*. How echoing that sense is if all one has come from has been so carried, literally, and one too is insistently "immigrant." As a child he memorized large chunks of Longfellow's *Hiawatha* in Yiddish, a fact that delighted his neighbors, the Italian bullies, who would plague him as he went to do errands and not stop till he'd recited enough to satisfy them. Punning itself is translation, a hearing of transposed meanings, by fact of sound. New York, one remembers, is the most polylingual city in the world. Translation has a very American quality even if no tradition, simply that Americans only speak English.

There is, however, a very different context for Zukofsky's use of translation, if one contrasts it with Pound's, for example, or almost any of the usual literary instances, such as Richmond Lattimore or Robert Graves. Zukofsky's first and abiding purchase on the text is its *sound*—much as if one were trying to enter the physical place of language, making sounds like "they" do, trying to inhabit the gestures, pace, and density of those ("objective") words. So these Catullus texts—which are, further, a collaboration between Celia Zukofsky and himself—manage a virtual sounding of the Latin (as reference to Catullus's Latin in any common collection will make clear), for example, "Ille mi par esse deo videtur" becomes "He'll hie me, par *is* he? the God divide her" (*LI*/51). The fascination is with system, but such "system" as can prove the increment of all that pertains, enters, "inclusive," as he said. It is the uniquely human attempt to "read" the world beyond one's own isolating proposal or simple control, so to enter into it, tenuous but explicit, from here to there and back again, from *I's* to *eyes*.

Zukofsky's life was spent for the most part in New York, where he felt most rooted and specific, whether it was the Lower East Side of his childhood, or Willow Street, Brooklyn, or finally on Central Park South. He taught many years at the Brooklyn Polytechnic Institute, which may have served his abiding respect for scientific qualification but frustrated his habits of generative speculation and reflection. His wife, Celia, said of him that he loved reading Spinoza as other men might love bread, and there is a deep kinship with Wittgenstein as with Aristotle, in that the world is to think, whether of or in or with. Friends such as Williams and Reznikoff were certainly there despite the public impression of a hermetic and increasingly isolated man. The fact of home, the domestic, became a center from which all might be projected and returned to. His love of Herrick is indicative, and in *A Test of Poetry*, under the rubric "Grace," one finds four poems of Herrick's, one each by Campion and Sir Francis Kynaston—all written between 1601 and 1648—with Zukofsky's "Little Wrists" (1948) their complement. More and more the young sought him out as a source for their own attempts to deal with an atrophied prosody, and many have so testified, such as Robert Duncan, Paul Blackburn, Cid Corman, Hugh Seidman, and the British poet Charles Tomlinson. His advice to Williams on the editing of the latter's collection *The Wedge* (1944) became a common highwater mark for the situation of his authority in and singular knowledge of the art. In like sense, Pound's earlier dedication of *Guide to Kulchur* (1938) to Bunting and Zukofsky was a useful signpost clearly so intended.

In 1972 the Zukofskys left the city to move to Port Jefferson, just above Stony Brook, where their son Paul was working at the State University of New York. No doubt that fact much persuaded them, but the increasing expense of their apartment was also a large reason. So, for the first time in some years, they were able to have a garden and also to find a range of wild flowers and herbs simply present in a way the city had precluded. Zukofsky's last work, then, a prospect for his eightieth birthday, has roots of literal kind. The poems of *80 Flowers* are so quiet, yet dense, with concentration, so echoing of all, himself included, where form follows and leads, a four times two, by fives—as eight lines, five words in each the count, no matter otherwise how much as syllable, translates, transforms, flowers to flower, in time as "thyme":

> Heart us invisibly thyme time
> round rose bud fire downland
> bird tread quagmire dry gill-over-the-ground
> stem-square leaves-cordate earth race horsethyme
> breath neighbors a mace nays
> sorrow of harness pulses pent

thus fruit pod split four
one-fourth *ripens* unwithering gaping

What end can there be? He might say otherwise, it is finally quite simple. Either you love or you hate. You have your life accordingly, "the more so all have it." When we first met, I felt nearly tongue-tied because I'd spent my last dime on the subway getting out to their home on Willow Street, Brooklyn, and now had to beg another to get back. To the ten cents was added five dollars, a lunch, and an overcoat I then wore for years. Later I'd come as I could and always found the same intensive warmth and response, a recognition so dear to my own tentative resources. There is a poem of mine called "The House," which is really Louis's—he took the baggage of my language and reduced it without threat to that compact, echoing sounding: "Mud put / upon mud / lifted / to make room." I've long forgotten what "the original" said.

Our last visit was after a chance meeting up near the park again. We arranged that I come the next afternoon and so I did, by subway, to find myself having to manage the last blocks in a wild summer thunderstorm. Thus I arrived as ever, in obvious need. Celia whisked my jacket into the bathroom and hung it up on the shower curtain rod to dry, and then I was given hot coffee. But I asked for milk, and there was none. So I was given a spoonful of vanilla ice cream in place of it, then some in a bowl in case that might please. To all of which, for all, there is hardly sufficient answer ever. Louis, I love you? So say these words.

ROBERT CREELEY

xiv

I Sent Thee Late
[1922]

I Sent Thee Late

Vast, tremulous;
Grave on grave of water-grave;

    Past.

Futurity no more than duration
Of a wave's rise, fall, rebound
Against the shingles, in ever repeated mutation
Of emptied returning sound.

55 Poems
[1923–1935]

اسرار جهان چنانکه در دفتر ماست

گفتن نتوان که آن وبال سر ماست

چون نیست درین مردم دانا اهلی

گفتن نتوان مر آنچه در خاطر ماست

عمر خیام

Omar Khayyám

Poem beginning "The"

Because I have had occasion to remember, quote, para-
phrase, I dedicate this poem to Anyone and Anything I have
unjustifiably forgotten. Also to J. S. Bach—309,* Bede's *Eccle-
siastical History*—248, 291, Max Beerbohm—245, Beethoven's
Ninth Symphony—310–312, Broadway—134, Geoffrey Chau-
cer—1st Movement, Title, College Cheer—45, E. E. Cum-
mings' *Is Five*—38, Dante—66, Norman Douglas' *South
Wind*—14, Elijah, the Prophet—24, T. S. Eliot's *The Waste
Land* and *The Sacred Wood*—25–27, John Erskine—184, 185,
Heinrich Heine—266, 267, 269, 316, Robert Herrick—187,
188, Horace—141, Horses—224–237, Aldous Huxley's *Those
Barren Leaves*—12, 18, Henry James—2nd Movement, Title,
Jewish Folk Song—191, 270–280, James Joyce—13, 20, 28, 29,
D. H. Lawrence—8, 19, 133, Christopher Marlowe's *Edward
II*—46, 47, Modern Advertising—163, George Moore—24,
Marianne Moore—22, Mussolini—74, 75, Myself—130, 142,
167, 309, Obvious—Where the Reference is Obvious, Walter
Pater's *Renaissance*—165, *Peer Gynt*—281–285, Poe's *Helen*—
168–182, Popular Non-Sacred Song—4, 5, 36, 37, 288, 289,
Ezra Pound—15, 18, Power of the Past, Present, and Fu-
ture—Where the reference is to the word Sun, E. A. Rob-
inson's *Children of the Night*—132, Sophocles—6, Oswald
Spengler—132, Max Stirner—199–202, Symbol of our Rela-
tively Most Permanent Self, Origin and Destiny—Wherever
the reference is to the word Mother, *The Bible*—1–3, 9, 313,
314, The Bolsheviki—203, 323, The French Language—31,
33, 51, 292, The King's English—166, *The Merchant of Ven-
ice*—250–265, The Yellow Menace—241–242, University Ex-
tension—70, Villon—21, Franz Werfel—68, Virginia Woolf's
Mrs. Dalloway—52, Yehoash—110–129, 205–223, 318–330.

*References following dashes are to lines in *Poem beginning "The."*

8

Poem beginning "The"

First Movement: *"And out of olde bokes, in good feith"*

1 The
2 Voice of Jesus I. Rush singing
3   in the wilderness
4 A boy's best friend is his mother,
5 It's your mother all the time.
6 Residue of Oedipus-faced wrecks
7 Creating out of the dead,—
8 From the candle flames of the souls of dead mothers
9 Vide the legend of thin Christ sending her
                    out of the temple,—
10 Books from the stony heart, flames rapping
                    the stone,
11 Residue of self-exiled men
12 By the Tyrrhenian.
13   Paris.
14 But everywhere only the South Wind, the
                    sirocco, the broken Earth-face.
15 The broken Earth-face, the age demands an
                    image of its life and contacts,
16 Lord, lord, not that we pray, are sure of
                    the question,
17 But why are our finest always dead?
18 And why, Lord, this time, is it Mauberley's
                    Luini in porcelain, why is it Chelifer,
19 Why is it Lovat who killed Kangaroo,
20 Why Stephen Dedalus with the cane of
                    ash,
21 But why les neiges?
22 And why, if all of Mary's Observations
                    have been made

23   Have not the lambs become more sapient
                  drinking of the spring;
24   Kerith is long dry, and the ravens that
                  brought the prophet bread
25   Are dust in the waste land of a raven-
                  winged evening.
26   And why if the waste land has been explored,
                  traveled over, circumscribed,
27   Are there only wrathless skeletons exhumed
                  new planted in its sacred wood,
28   Why—heir, long dead—Odysseus, wandering of ten years
29   Out-journeyed only by our Stephen, bibbing
                  of a day,
30   O why is that to Hecuba as Hecuba to he!

31   You are cra-a-zee on the subject of babies,
                  says she,
32   That is because somehow our authors have been
                  given a woman's intuition.
33   Il y a un peu trop de femme in this South Wind.
34   And on the cobblestones, bang, bang, bang,
                  myself like the wheels—
35   The tram passes singing
36   O do you take this life as your lawful wife,
37   I do!
38   O the Time is 5
39   I do!
40   O the Time is 5
41   I do!
42   O do you take these friends as your loves
                  to wive,
43   O the Time is 5
44   I do!

45   For it's the hoo-doos, the somethin' voo-doos
46   And not Kings onelie, but the wisest men
47   Graue Socrates, what says Marlowe?
48   For it was myself seemed held
49   Beating—beating—
50   Body trembling as over an hors d'oeuvres—
51

52 And the dream ending—Dalloway! Dalloway—
53 The blind portals opening, and I awoke!

54 Let me be
55 Not by art have we lived,
56 Not by graven images forbidden to us
57 Not by letters I fancy,
58 Do we dare say
59 With Spinoza grinding lenses, Rabbaisi,
60 After living on Cathedral Parkway?

Second Movement: *International Episode*

61 This is the aftermath
62 When Peter Out and I discuss the theatre.
63 Evenings, our constitutional.
64 We both strike matches, both in unison,
65   to light one pipe, my own.
66 'Tis, 'tis love, that makes the world go
              round and love is what I dream.
67 Peter is polite and I to me am almost as
              polite as Peter.
68 Somehow, in Germany, the Jew goat-song
              is unconvincing—
69   How the brain forms its visions think-
              ing incessantly of the things,
70 Not the old Greeks anymore,—
71   the things themselves a shadow world
              scarce shifting the incessant
              thought—
72 Time, time the goat were an offering,
73 Eh, what show do we see tonight, Peter?
74 "Il Duce: I feel God deeply."
75   Black shirts—black shirts—some power
              is so funereal.

76 Lion-heart, frate mio, and so on in two
              languages
77 the thing itself a shadow world.
78 Goldenrod

79 Of which he is a part,
80 Sod
81 He hurried over
82 Underfoot,
83 Make now
84 His testament of sun and sky
85 With clod
86 To root what shoot
87 It sends to run the sun,
88 The sun-sky blood.
89 My loves there is his mystery beyond
                      your loves.
90 Uncanny are the stars,
91 His slimness was as evasive
92 And his grimness was not yours,

93 Do you walk slowly the halls of the heavens,
94 Or saying that you do, lion-hearted not ours,
95 Hours, days, months, past from us and gone,
96 Lion-heart not looked upon, walk with the
                      stars.
97 Or have these like old men acknowledged
98 No kin but that grips of death,
99 Of being dying only to live on with them
100 Entirely theirs,
101 And so quickly grown old that we on earth like
                      stems raised dark
102 Feel only the lull, heave, phosphor
                      change, death, the
103 One follow, the other, the end?

104 Our candles have been buried beneath these
                      waters,
105 Their lights are his,
106 Ship-houses on the waters he might have lived
                      near.
107 Steady the red light and it makes no noise
                      whatever.
108 Damn it! they have made capital of his flesh
                      and bone.

109 What, in revenge, can dead flesh and bone
           make capital?
110 And his heart is dry
111 Like the teeth of a dead camel
112 But his eyes no longer blink
113 Not even as a blind dog's.

114 With the blue night shadows on the sand
115 May his kingdom return to him,
116 The Bedouin leap again on his *asilah*,
117 The expanse of heaven hang upon his shoulder
118 As an embroidered texture,
119 Behind him on his saddle sit the night
120 Sing into his ear:

121 Swifter than a tiger to his prey,
122 Lighter than the storm wind, dust or spray,
123 The Bedouin bears the Desert-Night,
124 Big his heart and young with life,
125 Younger yet his gay, wild wife
126   The Desert-Night.

127 Some new trappings for his steed,
128 All the stars in dowry his meed
129   From the Desert-Night.

130 I've changed my mind, Zukofsky,
131 How about some other show—
132 "The Queen of Roumania," "Tilbury,"
           "The West-Decline,"
133 "Hall's Mills," "The Happy Quetzal-
           coatl,"
134 "Near Ibsen," "Dancing with H. R. H.,"
           "Polly Wants a New Fur Coat,"
135 "The Post Office"—
136 Speaking of the post office, the following
           will handicap you for the position,
137   my dear peter,
138 Your weight less than one hundred
           twenty-five pounds,

139 One half of a disabled veteran, and
            probably
140   the whole of an unknown soldier,
141 That's indomitaeque morti for you.

142 Is it true what you say, Zukofsky,
143 Sorry to say, My Peter Out.

144 "Tear the Codpiece Off, A Musical
            Comedy,"
145 Likewise, "Panting for Pants,"
146 "The Dream That Knows No Waking."

Third Movement: *In Cat Minor*

147 Hard, hard the cat-world.
148 On the stream Vicissitude
149 Our milk flows lewd.

150 We'll cry, we'll cry,
151 We'll cry the more
152 And wet the floor,

153 Megrow, megrow,
154 Around around
155 The only sound

156 The prowl, our prowl,
157 Of gentlemen cats
158 With paws like spats

159 Who weep the nights
160 Till the nights are gone—
161 —And r-r-run—the Sun!

Fourth Movement: *More "Renaissance"*

162 Is it the sun you're looking for,
163 Drop in at Askforaclassic, Inc.,

164 Get yourself another century,
165 A little frost before sundown,
166 It's the times don'chewknow,
167 And if you're a Jewish boy, then be your
         Plato's Philo.

168 Engprof, thy lectures were to me
169   Like those roast flitches of red boar
170 That, smelling, one is like to see
171   Through windows where the steam's galore
172   Like our own "Cellar Door."

173 On weary bott'm long wont to sit,
174   Thy graying hair, thy beaming eyes,
175 Thy heavy jowl would make me fit
176   For the Pater that was Greece.
177   The siesta that was Rome.

178 Lo! from my present—say not—itch
179   How statue-like I see thee stand
180 Phi Beta Key within thy hand!
181   Professor—from the backseats which
182 Are no man's land!

183 Poe,
184 Gentlemen, don'chewknow,
185 But never wrote an epic.

Fifth Movement: *Autobiography*

186 Speaking about epics, mother,
187 How long ago is it since you gathered
         mushrooms,
188 Gathered mushrooms while you mayed.
189 Is it your mate, my father, boating.
190 A stove burns like a full moon in a desert night.
191 Un in hoyze is kalt. You think of a new
         grave,
192 In the fields, flowers.

193 Night on the bladed grass, bayonets dewed.
194 Is it your mate, my father, boating.
195 Speaking about epics, mother,—
196 Down here among the gastanks, ruts,
          cemetery-tenements—
197 It is your Russia that is free.
198 And I here, can I say only—
199   "So then an egoist can never embrace
              a party
200   Or take up with a party?
201   Oh, yes, only he cannot let himself
202   Be embraced or taken up by the party."
203 It is your Russia that is free, mother.
204 Tell me, mother.

205 Winged wild geese, where lies the passage,
206 In far away lands lies the passage.
207 Winged wild geese, who knows the pathway?
208 Of the winds, asking, we shall say:
209 Wind of the South and wind of the North
210 Where has our sun gone forth?
211 Naked, twisted, scraggly branches,
212 And dark, gray patches through the branches,
213 Ducks with puffed-up, fluttering feathers
214 On a cobalt stream.
215 And faded grass that's slowly swaying.
216 A barefoot shepherd boy
217 Striding in the mire:
218 Swishing indifferently a peeled branch
219 On jaded sheep.
220 An old horse strewn with yellow leaves
221 By the edge of the meadow
222 Draws weakly with humid nostrils
223 The moisture of the clouds.
224 Horses that pass through inappreciable
          woodland,
225 Leaves in their manes tangled, mist, autumn
          green,
226 Lord, why not give these bright brutes—
          your good land—
227 Turf for their feet always, years for their mien.

228 See how each peer lifts his head, others follow,
229 Mate paired with mate, flanks coming full
           they crowd,
230 Reared in your sun, Lord, escaping each hollow
231 Where life-struck we stand, utter their praise
           aloud.
232 Very much Chance, Lord, as when you first
           made us,
233 You might forget them, Lord, preferring what
234 Being less lovely where sadly we fuss?
235 Weed out these horses as tho they were not?
236 Never alive in brute delicate trembling
237 Song to your sun, against autumn assembling.

238 If horses could but sing Bach, mother,—
239 Remember how I wished it once—
240 Now I kiss you who could never sing Bach,
           never read Shakespeare.

241 In Manhattan here the Chinamen are yellow
           in the face, mother,
242 Up and down, up and down our streets they
           go yellow in the face,
243 And why is it the representatives of your,
           my, race are always hankering for
           food, mother?
244 We, on the other hand, eat so little.
245 Dawn't you think Trawtsky rawthaw a
           darrling,
246 I ask our immigrant cousin querulously.
247 Naw! I think hay is awlmawst a Tchekoff.
248 But she has more color in her cheeks than
           the Angles—Angels—mother,—
249 They have enough, though. We should
           get some more color, mother.
250 If I am like them in the rest, I should
           resemble them in that, mother,
251 Assimilation is not hard,
252 And once the Faith's askew
253 I might as well look Shagetz just as much
           as Jew.

254   I'll read their Donne as mine,
255   And leopard in their spots
256   I'll do what says their Coleridge,
257   Twist red hot pokers into knots.
258   The villainy they teach me I will execute
259   And it shall go hard with them,
260   For I'll better the instruction,
261   Having learned, so to speak, in their
        colleges.
262   It is engendered in the eyes
263   With gazing fed, and fancy dies
264   In the cradle where it lies
265   In the cradle where it lies
266   I, Senora, am the Son of the Respected
        Rabbi,
267   Israel of Saragossa,
268   Not that the Rabbis give a damn,
269   Keine Kadish wird man sagen.

Half-dozenth Movement: *Finale, and After*

270   Under the cradle the white goat stands, mother,
271   What will the goat be saddled with, mother?
272   Almonds, raisins
273   What will my heart be bartering, mother,
274   Wisdom, learning.
275   Lullaby, lullaby, lullaby, lullaby.
276   These are the words of the prophet, mother,
277   Likely to save me from Tophet, mother—
278   What will my heart be burning to, mother,
279   Wisdom, learning.
280   By the cat and the well, I swear, my
        Shulamite!
281   In my faith, in my hope, and in my love.
282   I will cradle thee, I will watch thee,
283   Sleep and dream thou, dear my boy!
284   (Presses his cheek against her mouth.)
285   I must try to fare forth from here.
286   I do not forget you,
287   I am just gone out for to-night,

288 The Royal Stag is abroad,
289 I am gone out hunting,
290 The leaves have lit by the moon.
291 Even in their dirt, the Angles like Angels
       are fair,
292 Brooks Nash, for instance, faisant un petit
       bruit, mais très net,
293 Saying, He who is afraid to do that should
       be denied the privilege,
294 And where the automobile roads with the
       gasoline shine,
295 Appropriately the katydid—
296 Ka-ty did . . . . Ka-ty didn't . . . .

297 Helen Gentile,
298 And did one want me; no.
299 But wanted me to take one? yes.
300 And should I have kissed one? no.
301 That is, embraced one first
302 And holding closely one, then kissed one?
       yes.
303 Angry against things' iron I ring
304 Recalcitrant prod and kick.
305 Oh, Baedekera Schönberg, you here
306   dreaming of the relentlessness of motion
307 As usual,
308 One or two dead in the process what does it
       matter.

309 Our God immortal such Life as is our God,
310 Bei dein Zauber, by thy magic I embrace
       thee,
311 Open Sesame, Ali Baba, I, thy firefly, little
       errant star, call here,
312 By thy magic I embrace thee.

313 O my son Sun, my son, my son Sun!
       would God
314 I had died for thee, O Sun, my son, my
       son!

315 I have not forgotten you, mother,—
316 It is a lie—Aus meinen grossen leiden mach ich
        die kleinen lieder,
317 Rather they are joy, against nothingness joy—
318 By the wrack we shall sing our Sun-song
319 Under our feet will crawl
320 The shadows of dead worlds,
321 We shall open our arms wide,
322 Call out of pure might—
323 Sun, you great Sun, our Comrade,
324 From eternity to eternity we remain true to you,
325 A myriad years we have been,
326 Myriad upon myriad shall be.

327 How wide our arms are,
328 How strong,
329 A myriad years we have been,
330 Myriad upon myriad shall be.

29 POEMS

1
Memory of V. I. Ulianov

Immemorial,
And after us
Immemorial,
O white
O orbit-trembling,
Star, thru all the leaves
Of elm;—
Lighted-one, beyond the trunk tip
Of the elm
High, proportionately vast,
Of mist and form;—
Star, of all live processes
Continual it seems to us,
Like elm leaves,
Lighted in your glow;—
We thrive in strange hegira
Here below,
Yet sometimes in our flight alone
We speak to you,
When nothing that was ours seems spent
And life consuming us seems permanent,
And flight of stirring beating up the night
And down and up; we do not sink with every wave.
Travels our consciousness
Deep in its egress.
Eclipsed the earth, for earth is power
And we of earth.
Eclipsed our death, for death is power
And we of death.
Single we are, tho others still may be with us
And we for others.
We have come to the sources of being,
Inviolable, throngs everlasting, rising forever,
Rush as of river courses,
Change within change of forces.
Irrevocable yet safe we go,

Irrevocable you, too,
O star, we speaking to you,
The shadows of the elm leaves faded,
Only the trunk of elm now dark and high
Unto your height:
Now and again you fall,
Blow dark and burn again,
And we in turn
Share now your fate
Whose process is continual.

2

Not much more than being,
Thoughts of isolate, beautiful
Being at evening, to expect
                    at a river-front:

A shaft dims
With a turning wheel;

Men work on a jetty
By a broken wagon;

Leopard, glowing-spotted,
    The summer river—
Under: The Dragon:

3

Cocktails
and signs of
"ads"

flashing,
light's waterfalls,

Bacchae
among electric lights

will swarm the crowds
streamers of the lighted

skyscrapers

nor tripping
over underbrush

but upon pavement

and not with thyrsus
shall they prick

the body of their loves
but waist to waist

laugh out in gyre—
announced then upon stairs,

not upon hills,
will be their flight

when passed turnstiles,
having dropped

coins
they've sprinted up

where on the air (elevated)
waves flash—and out—

leap
signaling—lights below

4

Buoy—no, how,
It is not a question: what
Is this freighter carrying?—
Did smoke blow?—That whistle?—

Of course, commerce will not complete
Anything, yet the harbor traffic is busy,
                there shall be a complete fragment

Of—

Nothing, look! that gull
Streak the water!
Getting nearer are we,
Hear? count the dissonances,

Shoal? accost—cost
Cost accounting.

5
Ferry

Gleams, a green lamp
In the fog:
Murmur, in almost
A dialogue

Siren and signal
Siren to signal.

Parts the shore from the fog,
Rise there, tower on tower,
Signs of stray light
And of power.

Siren to signal
Siren to signal.

Hour-gongs and the green
Of the lamp.

Plash. Night. Plash. Sky.

6

How many
Times round

Deck, ladies?

What says
The nigger?

"Fi' minutes
After a

Man's breath
Leaves

His body
He knows—'

Much 'bout
Himself 's

Ten years
Befo' 'e

Was bo'n—"

What you
Say to

That, ladies?

The Statue
Of Liberty's

Drunk?!
French! !

7
During the Passaic Strike of 1926

the sexton of the rich parish of St. Mark's-on-the-Bouwerie, New York, imparted the news to my friend, S.T.H., that there was only room for two in his graveyard.

There are two vaults left in St. Mark's-on-the-Bouwerie,
There are two vaults left to bury the dead,
O when the two vaults are filled in St. Mark's-on-the-Bouwerie,
How will the dead bury their dead?

For Justice they are shrewdly killing the proletarian,
For Justice they are shrewdly shooting him dead,
Good Heavens, when the vaults are filled in St. Mark's-on-the-
Bouwerie,
How will the dead bury their dead!

("I was born indeed in your dominions, but your service was hard, and your wages such as a man could not live on"—Pilgrim's Progress.)

8

And to paradise which is a port
And over water-trestle,
And as over a sea so over: and by the way
of this train's movement

Water-staves,
Moorings, spread blue coats of water,
Long,
Along,
Long.

9

A dying away as of trees
        where a hill-street pavement
        is broken into rocks:

A car sounds,

        Climbs.
     Empty, late Saturday.

At the bottom of the grade
        stopped short in one's rounds
        this tree-dying night of hurrying towards Sunday,
            uptorn by an empty trolley's rumble on usual
                                  pursuits,
          retreats to meet
          street after empty street,
          hills paved, rising to be climbed,
          and what for houses but for windows?
          sure forecast of ongrowing moonlight.

10

          Passing tall
          Who walk upon the green
          So light they are not heard
          If never seen;—

          Willow above in spring haze,
          Green sprig and pendulous;—
          Wind, white lightning
          In branches over us;

          Sun;
          All weathering changing loves,
          In the high grass (kiss!)
          Will not uncover us.

11

Stubbing the cloud-fields—the searchlight, high
In the roseate twilight of rain-sky, green! green spring
In the heavens mild in the spring; or down suddenly
Earthwards, plunge deep suddenly earthwards,
Like escape, stampede of cattle horns, ghastly, ghastly
Their giant heads invisible for joy, grief, cavalcade,
                                    plunge earthwards,
And into our hearts, O sacrifice,
But we emerge! (emerge upon a level roof that fronts
                                    the sky,
The skylight of your room to rear,)
So we can breathe, the rain air and the spring
Ours, till again it moves along the sky
Down or up, machine-rayed, powerful!

12

Millennium of sun—
Beast of the field,—
Kissing the beast upon both ears—

O who will pluck geranium
With smiles before this ass's face
And tie it to his cranium
To match the ass's grace!

13

We are crossing the bridge now.
I can feel it by the sound
The wheels make over the waters.
To-night we cannot see
From the windows. But there are lights
Of two shores. And if you open the door
The water-wind blows in the brume
Which covers us.

14

Only water—

We seek of the water
The water's love!

Shall we go again
Breast to water-breast,

Gather the fish-substance,
The shining fire,
The phosphor-subtlety?

We sing who were many in the South,
At each live river mouth
Sparse-lighted, carried along!

15

And looking to where shone Orion,
Wickson—"The miracle were done
If she were to bear my son.

"As to taste there's no dispute.
But who is he may taste?
These miles of beach—
Coarse grass and ocean waste—

"Where on them can I get,
Or from their green of stars,
Something like a cucumber?"

16
Aubade, 1925

Kick the blanket away,
The man of darkness has sweated enough!
One, two, three efforts, and he stands on his feet—
Chilled a little on the cold sands.

Day. Still he is blinking man,
But eyes open: he sees
The sea, little waves, waves of the morning pearl-gray!

Agh! running the wind!

But think with the head!
This is the state of man
To raise his ashes to the dawn.
Jump, away from the coast-guard house,
Across one, two, three—! Sand mounds,

And a swamp,
Crosses of wood, newspapers in coarse island grass,
Behind a hill to be as simple as the horses.

Who has seen, who can, and who will ever see?
No one about but flat island sand and flat blue sky and
        a few mounds
Behind which—the sea, its reverberations.
Whence, if ever, then, will come sympathy?
Surely not out of the sun, nor out of the sky,
Nor out of eternity of flat island sand a little lowly to
      the aspect of eternal morning.

                    Orbed sun! great air! slow time!
                    The man of darkness
                    Is his own monument,
                    Moving his return—

Bah-h! so much blanket again—
Tousled hair—sleep!

Swims!
Spewing and spewn on to the land!
                    The sun is hot!

17

Cars once steel and green, now old,
Find their grave at Cedar Manor.
They rust in a wind
The sky alone can hold.

For the wind
Flows heavily thru the mind like cold,
Drums in the ears
Till one knows its being which soon is not.

18

Tall and singularly dark you pass among the breakers—
Companionship as of another world bordering on this;
To the intelligence fastened by the senses you are lost
In a world of sunlight where nothing is amiss:

For nothing but the sun is there and peace vital with the sun,
The heaviest changes shift through no feature more than a smile,
Currents spread, and are gone, and as the high waves appear,
You dive, in the calming are as lost awhile.

How in that while intelligence escapes from sense
And fear with hurled human might darkens upon bliss!
Till as again you stand above the waters
Fear turns to sleep as one who dreamt of falling, an abyss!

19

Run on, you still dead to the sound of a name:
Climb, white froth, as on stems of flowers;

Pass near the curve of the heavens.
Sunned your whiteness is of winter frost.

For you, froth, the surge of blue-sweeping autumn,
Run to the gate of the snowed winter tomb
Where none ask why the death nor for whom;

Where the sun, too, grows small and of winter—
Drifted fruit, rotten.—

20

Close your eyes,
                        the sun low—upon them

Sky grows down, one petal
Daisy petal, broad, luminous.
A wind that makes for blindness—
                        Sun

21

O sleep, the sky goes down behind the poplars,
I scrape the gravel with my shoes and toe
The ties:
The milky moon is in the clearing,
Only the power-plant hurries in winter.

22

Cactus rose-mauve and gray, twin overturned
　　　　natural play-paniers
in a burnt little earthen pot, green mortuary
　　　　of plainness.
Cactus minus the red bud flower,
and the same day
　　　　nescience of treading knee deep in snow,
always mortmain the oblivion of her
　　　　in the desert of my traces—
Hannah, "grace." Grace under the moon,
　　　　on blue velvet cloth I placed the prickly plant.

Think of snow.
Know duration.
All once grafted hers go to her,
　　　　the plants, too, unseen continuance.

23
Song Theme

*To the last movement of Beethoven's Quartet
in C Sharp Minor*

All my days—
And all my ways—
Met by hands—
And ringed with feet—
Into laurel-branch the hands
Are gone, into fertile soil the feet;
　　　　So these praised ones that are fallen off
　　　　Are a signal in the trees,
　　　　Are a beacon in the sun,—

　　　　Sun and death and stir, and death's
　　　　　　　　　unlit love,—
　　　　All their days
　　　　And all their ways.

24
tam cari capitis

I

Unlovely you called yourself
And at once I felt I was never lovely:
I, who had few truths to go to
Found you doubting what I loved.

Now I make you lovely my own way.
Unmentioned were we certain
Of a greater, in small assurances
Others may find trivial:

II

The same in all weathers.

And not till there is an end to singing
Will you go,
As you have always gone, quiet.

But like your birds that wake in the night
To sleep again:

25

Like the oceans, or the leaves of fine Southern
      palm, we must appear numbered
         to you, like the tides

Reaching up to you, also as leaves, calm, night-green,
      arching under you,
      Moon. And, O moon,
As we travail to sleep we do not know whether, with your
      genius furthering us,

We should be counted as the cuspid waves of the seas, or
as the souls of trees
Whose leaves we are, growing for you, the crowded
summits stark, heavenly.

26

Ask of the sun
and it may tell you—

if it will come
if it has come

that afternoon
of afternoons

when you'll have ended
shaping a plaything

circus horse of glass
a mane of beads

since art's high effort
vying with the sun's heat

shadows small—
when rather like thick peasants

out of Brueghel
after working

you stretch out—
the sun among

the hayricks of Its fields
and artless find time.

Blue light is the night harbor-slip.
If a number are gold they make a crown for the shore.
If three rise vertically, as one nethermost, another
over that, another topping,
All as if reaching, the vessel is making headway.

The scarf-pins of night-outers are sometimes that way
And, God's sky! if the body of something deploys one
gold light for'ard,
And, shy, a smile, may it be named? another gold light
as trailer,
The general 'it is after midnight' may be a marriage,
or a return from the month's ball.

Masquerade, Mozart,
Filigree—they used to—

(We had such a nice time)

Red! look out for this island!

Blue! and it hurts the eyes, metallic-glass this
beacon-light, many-faceted

It is generally safer here because,
in the white-washed ceiling hulk,
not only sparse lights for the deck
but life-belts

Danger! The general effect of gray light in darkness
is a man-of-war

Red!

Out far again
Lights—a branch laid on the world—
Their intermittence—

(We look abroad openly)

28 & 29
Two Dedications

Tibor Serly

Red varnish
Warm flitch

Of cello,
They play

Scroll before
Them—Sound

Breaks the
Sunset!—Kiss

With wide
Eyes—With

Their music
The (no?)

Pit, weather
Of tears

Which plagues
Us—Bodies

Of waves
Whose crests

Spear air,
Here rolls

The sea—
Go chase

It—a
Salt pact

Ranged over
Bars—white

Ribs pervade
In constant

Measures the
Rounds—Its

Wet frosting,
A kiss

Opens nothing,
Bend head

No! lips
Not this

An assumed
Poise among

Crowds! Blue—
Withdraws sunset—

Tones sound—
Pluck—dissonant—

Stops sing
The welter

D.R.

Comrade D.R.—
His murals speak:
Executives of industry,

Rich stone heads
Conferring at tables,
We peasants and

Workers, our faces
Becoming us more
Than frescoes of saints,

Marshal to say:
We are the
Heads over industry.

Our children, (backs
Pretty as lady bugs,
Red upon gold

Soil) now humbled
On stumps, grow
Up on soil

Turning black thru
Our efforts—water,
Our biceps, unspared.

Our mates, their mothers,
Shall know them—
Unflattered by dynamos—

Controlled among wheels
And controlling the
Glancing of belts

Against pulleys, Holidays—
There'll be many—
Will find friends

Rangers among palm
Leaf and tiger
Paw.

    Sunday; the
Miner's lantern unlit,
Coal beneath sun.

29 SONGS

1
Madison, Wis.,
remembering the bloom of Monticello (1931)

No empty bed blues—
    between these walls
I can lie—
    your thigh, me—

"Keep in it deer,
    rabbits, pigeons"—
"the figure will be better
    placed in this,"—

"Form a couch of moss"—
    queer guy
Tom Jefferson—all daughters
    no son

Sure, if you wish
    we can
turn the small Alleghenies
    to upper Japan—

But if Mr. citizen
    sells apples
in New York by
    the sea

Maybe that's
    where we
should be—
    I'll die—

The heart all
    a queen's
the brain
    Lenin's—

Empty Bed
    Blues—"keep the
thorn constantly
   wed."

2
Immature Pebbles

An Imponderable is an article of make-believe which has become
axiomatic by force of settled habit. It can accordingly cease to be an
Imponderable by a course of unsettling habit.
                           —Thorstein Veblen

There are several robins here,
their legs among the triple buds—
the spring is yet too brisk
for water suds, (bathers' dirt):
instead, where the trees almost
into the water grow—below them
over the split moistened stones, ripples
make for? An observer's irrelevancy
                 of April.
Following: May.

Should then this repeated objectless
of inconsequence, following and May
bring the expected to the accustomed
in this place,
the surprise will, it can be seen, not exceed
legs of young men and women
bathing in a lake—
summer's inaction colored hot—
blue and crimson of their shivering suits
among the trees, no less ironic than what male,
encaged mandrill's blue and crimson
secret parts?

Observer, then, come get one going,
before one's an accessory to these ways,
obliged to accept "imponderables"—
those axioms of settling habits

no less, no more, attractive than a lake's inclusions—
pebbles, young humans . . .
In our day, impatience
handles such matters of photography
more pertinently from a train window.

3
Prop. LXI

*(The Strength of The Emotions—Ethica ordine
geometrico demonstrata: IV)*

Confute leaf-
Point's water with slight dropped sounds,—
Turn coat, cheat facts, say for the spring's bloom's fall
The tree's trunk has set the circling horn-branch
To cipher each drop—the eye—shot in the rain around.

So cheated well
Let the fallen bloom-wet clutter down, and into . . .
And the heart (fact . .) holds nothing, desire is
No excess, the eye points each leaf
The brain desire, the rain (cheat.) recites their brief.

4
Train-Signal

With stars past troughs to sound
—thru thick twilight
—by the stumps of the trees
blasts near the faces of leaves
by a hair's breadth separated:

with but a proof to the leaves'
closeness: leaf over leaf's face
with a hair: and the cheek kissed
with the shredded space.

5
It's a gay li - ife

There's naw—thing
    lak po—ee try
it's a delicacy
    for   a horse:

Dere's na—thing
    lak pea-   nut-brittle
it's a delicacy
    for   the molars.

6
—"her soil's birth"

(Madison)

Virtue in that—
If fall of pods' spring-seed to earth,
    Sun, ferns rise at,
Together glassed themselves in green, girth
With the windfall of her soil's birth.

    Rays sent from glass
Sphering with its beamed fall the air
    Could not surpass—
Designed to meet opposed beams there—
The unsealing of the eyes bare.

Explosions such
As these are not for eyes to prink:
    Pods' fall too much
Inevitable, each pod will sink
Its green into a glass we drink.—

43

Spring's air! which keeps
The sharpest rays of sun askew—
          Over pods sweeps:
Flecks green her hands—like ferns' virtue
In the sun keeping their green true.

7

Who endure days like this
with me   the room's inference
foghorns' tuned discs amiss
dropped our wrists would be
seconds   impatience' stem
gestures' graft   arms difference
eyes' blue iris splicing them

8

Happier, happier, now
For whom in snowsleet barberries see;
          If not that, if not that, how
Are red berries for their windsleights free?
The glaze of mind, winter of eyes,
          Snow's berries, meet!
The Void of mind, the fall of thighs,
          Cold winds heat.

          Yellow flowers dead, green of leaves
Still green, look out of what eyes in love's Void?
          The close, the unseeing and unseen,
The glaze of sight snowsleet has destroyed.
Windblown, for all barberries not dead
          See with love's tear,—
The fall of thighs; love's discrete forehead
          Happier.

9

In Arizona
          (how many years in the mountains)
The small stumped bark of a tree
Looks up
          in the shape of an adored pup

The indians do not approach it
The round indian tents
          remain where they are
The tanned whites
          are never seen by it
And one can imagine its imploring eyes

The skies
          it seems to look up to
                              blue
The same sun that warms the desert
Warms what one
          can imagine to be its ears.

10
Arizona

          arch animals'
          upearthed faces—
          dust of
          their red, wrinkled—

          higher than the oil wells
          are the rocks—
          the fluted cactus, its
          spiked needle locks,

          rasp shard in
          the blue air, blood boil
          into the unprofitable
          eiffel towers of oil

11
Home for Aged Bomb Throwers—U.S.S.R.

When is winter spring?
When, tho ice is not breaking,
One has what one does not expect
    to be taking

It is against the winds
It is against firm ice
But with the sun, that
        falling asleep
Winter is spring

1/6 of the earth

12

Whatever makes this happening
   Is unheard
   To a third.

Two. Where two should
   Stand. One. One.
   With the sun. In a wood.

Tomorrow is unsought.
   No oasis of ivy to inurn
   Either foot or fern.

13

in that this happening
   is not unkind
it put to
   shame every kindness

mind, mouths, their words
people, put sorrow
on
its body

before sorrow it came
and before every kindness,
happening for every sorrow
before every kindness;

14

The sand: For the cigarette finished
on the beach the universal ash-tray:

or where the bacon grease is spilt:
Knowledge: smell is taken up

and off by the seas'
winds:

a ship's
funnel is seen from this house
and rain drenches a witness of departure:

love as the relaxation among breakers
a dog-carcass—its wet—a reminder:

15

Do not leave me
before that convert surfeit
which if it ever leaves toward you—
never to your misgiving—
inexistent
comes first to me in another

That surfeit—other—which
    much less you do not look for, distraction
from this our being together
    never surfeit—the owned
devolving upon—owned—and neither owned—

That distraction which neither of us
    much less you, close, seeks—love
never prior to your patience
    asks that surfeit come upon me first—
unowned misgiving;

it is but a mouth's mumblings:
    no distraction coming
after love, convert
    of your patience—a mouth knowing;
close, its unowned owner.

16

    Crickets'
    thickets

    light,
    delight:

    sleeper's eyes,
    keeper's;

        Plies!
    lightning

    frightening
    whom . . . ?

    doom
    nowhere . . .

where eyes   .   .   .
air,

are crickets'
air

17
Imitation*

N.Y. 1932

In the imitation of Gothic
building   and a virgin
as Virgin   her recessed space
Her alcove   its "statue"   a quadrangle
stones considered built   imitation
within a court   a garden   bluebells
in New York City   imitation of
a chalet   set apart for meals
familiar to Americans if not the Swiss

this institution   by deliberateness   of engraving
THE   ACADEMY   OF   THE   HOLY   CHILD
to which dedicated from up
the rich street hurries   promised   young
the academician and wholly child
all his attention religiously kept by vast
cubic contents of gas tank built on principles of
a steel erector set given him by his aunt
just off the boat from Pekin   coloration of sea
plate steel rectangles mirrored blue at the water-line
the gas tank walls   the same composition   same color

—Xavier   you know, or have not you heard
in China even comparatively recently
the physicians attending women of the upper
class never saw their patients but for
a hand extended from behind a screen
for the taking of their pulse   and so   depended
for the rest of the diagnoses upon a proxy

49

a small carved figure of a woman
sometimes of ivory upon which the patient indicated
the approximate location of her complaint

other Chinese ivories   tablets which were held
in front of their mouths by officials
when they had audience   certain leaves
fall long crisp like red halved sausages
roasted to a turn this autumn for the sidewalks
of New York of the occupants of the taxis
of the imitation of wealth thru the exhaust
girdle pendants   back scratchers with ivory handles
cages for singing and fighting crickets

*Imitation: *Mus.* The repetition of a phrase or subject in another
voice-part or in a different key.

18

The mirror oval sabres   playing

at chips in the room

next door   the voices behind the wall

will be lit by high lights in the morning

in bed a wall between continuing voices

chips stacking   instead of bales

the water sounds extending a harbor

one sleepless one sleeper on the fourth floor

19

Checkers, checkmate and checkerboard,
Confused are *checkerboard* and *chess*;
Shall whose writing be on paper
Whose move is on the checkerboard?

If red of a set have each a wreath
Each black checker should be wreathed:
Noble typing will make the writing
Her breath is his, to type "checkmate bequeathed."

20

Ears beringed with fuzz

owned a man's sculpturing head

autumn's regard

                      for weather like spring

holed shoes meeting pavement

If, when,

           introduce these to

a fuzzed flower   Petal will

declare as of carving   "bluish soles'

walk, head, ears' hair: greeting"

21

Snows' night's winds on the window rattling
Would seem to leap out of the bed-spring

What prevents a feat like that occurring
Reason—but the more actual bedding

Springs of steel mercurial spirallings
Making a body's night a changeable singing

The winged boots of the frozen seek of it! sheltering
Safety from the window's pommelling

22

To my wash-stand
in which I wash
my left hand
and my right hand

To my wash-stand
whose base is Greek
whose shaft
is marble and is fluted

To my wash-stand
whose wash-bowl
is an oval
in a square

To my wash-stand
whose square is marble
and inscribes two
smaller ovals to left and right for soap

Comes a song of
water from the right faucet and the left
my left and my
right hand mixing hot and cold

Comes a flow which
if I have called a song
is a song
entirely in my head

a song out of imagining
modillions descried above
my head   a frieze
of stone completing what no longer

is my wash-stand
since its marble has completed
my getting up each morning
my washing before going to bed

          my look into a mirror
to glimpse half an oval
          as if its half
were half-oval in my head   and the

          climates of many
inscriptions human heads shapes'
          horses' elephants' (tusks) others'
scratched in marble tile

          so my wash-stand
in one particular breaking of the
          tile at which I have
looked and looked

          has opposed to my head
the inscription of a head
          whose coinage is the
coinage of the poor

          observant in waiting
in their getting up mornings
          and in their waiting
going to bed

          carefully attentive
to what they have
          and to what they do not
              have

when a flow of water
          doubled in narrow folds
occasions invertible counterpoints
          over a head   and

          an age in a wash-stand
and in their own heads

23
"The Immediate Aim"

1

Other than propaganda—

a police dog sniffs one;
a *German* police dog
not responsible for Naziism?
One is not sweet on him.

When one does not love animals,
one's concern is not respect.

Workers,
you could
take time off
this March morning

trot out
like this police dog

ambling critic
of spring

(the curse of verse on him!)

might make bare your eyes
to the white gull
astigmatically a launch

since it sits, distant
in the middle of the river:

your value which enslaves you
in advance

has made your eye-pupils limited—

inanity
to prate
the injustice of it.

2

Can dogs
argue
injustices

Dogs in a vise,
and a wood saw
can saw an anatomy
of dog

Such as you never saw.

If it yowls
shut the eyelid on a bad dream,
Let not the snarls take,
With its virus in you
You are immune.

What hounds
you means to.
Not all woodsawyers
grow animal.

3

Shanty
on the river
with
one window

The unemployed
having
a home
has no home

55

and no nag
protected
by
the United States' flag—

each animal
his own gravedigger
almost
sings

who will
walk out
against
the

social
and political
order of
things

24
This Fall, 1933

THE AMERICAN BANKNOTE FACTORY
    makes bills
The lights are on thru its basement,
    10 times 10 squared down the windows of its façade.

A boy with a rabbit in hand could no more
Caress it for his benumbed fingers, than if
    The drafts from the outside blew in noon and midnight,

Stormed green bills on the fall's leaves, the bills
Could caress them, make New York pavement less
    Bereavement, heyday out of moneyed inflation.

25
No One Inn

P.S.   i.e.   almost dreamt
the face against the door
a pastel's   a boy's

who owns it   being in a war
plays the market early
hires a chef   would look at his chef's hat

flour not at the exchange of
the exchanges   the margin drops
gets the chef walking   and preparing

it a cork   please,
be it, whose thought is it
floated   and by a house-boat

if there   wound's sleep, to be sure
"then bacteria in mercurochrome?"—yes
if you want peroxide I will give you—thrive

the windings   an inn
the windings   a face in an inn
the windings   no one is in in No One Inn

26
A Junction

To such of one body as one mind

Whose ear shouts to ear separation,

Across the mean levels of oceans,

     Cities,—

To them a sight thru windows

Which will not last,

The heart, and an arm—if it should conduct

Remembering.

27
Song—¾ time
(*pleasantly drunk*)

Right out
      of
           Das Kapital

vol. I
      chap. 3
           2.
              A

"who has
      a
           taste

"for something
           that will
                warm
                    up"

snow
      for
           my friend's birthday

I've
      been climbing
                every
                    little

highway
        snow without—
                    He

dances
        it
        —without—
                    any money

(his
    friend's
            nose

is
  at
    the
        window

for the
        snow
                sparrows

in the
        junk
            heap
                of snow)

with
    a
    girl

over
    every
        little
                highway

of
  Spain
        for—

"there
        develops
                a
                    multiplicity

"of
    social
            relations

"that are
            spontaneous in
                                their
                                        growth

"and are
            quite
                    outside

"the
        control of
                    the
                        actors"

"When
        one commodity
                        replaces another

"the
    money
            commodity
                        always

"remains
        in
            the hands

"of
    some
        third
                person"

"Circulation

       sweats money

              unceasingly

"at every pore."

        "because the

            weaver has sold

                 linen;

"the distiller

       is only able to

           sell the strong

"waters

     because the

         bible agent has already

"sold the waters

       of

       —

      life;

"and

  so

    on."

28

"Specifically, a writer of music." The composite of notes proceeded with assumed qualities in a definite proportion. But, as dreamed, they controlled the nature of plants, bodies, etc., and the elements of the notes became not easy to separate. And, on the large muscle of the back, which passes from the spine to the head, they were settled longitudinally, like the wings of certain insects, where in the large opening of the roof in the ancient house stood the air.

He stood and turned the palm of the hand downward and backward, and like the notes the movement was extended in time. This act became a test of his powers. His body was published abroad, and like the Titan, long after him, whose liver renewed itself at night, it renewed itself on a long promenade in the mornings of days, the notes always the principal effort of his performance. He saw no one—only flowers, branches and buds developing from unusual places.

Till where the stamens combined by their filaments to form two bundles, he saw her, the power of authority upon her head. But her crown was a crown of his notes, so that she was immediately separate from him, as the notes were separate from her in what seemed to him their conversation in which she did yet did not take part. She disappeared into the brush.

And he heard himself saying, "For, I am at least half blind, my windows are all as full of glasses of waters as any mountebanks stall" on a field crowded with dancing donkeys. Half-crazed, he was running into them, seeking always the daughter of the governor of Seville. Stamping over him, the hoofs of the donkeys delivered, themselves delivered, the body of Don Giovanni to the devil. And as the field was impaired upon the point of their receding vision, the ever falling stomping of their hoofs, now following the range of his notes, were imparting to him clearly: "Sir, not only a mathematique point flowers into every line which is derived from a Center, but our soul which is but one, hath swallowed up a negative."

And now a dancing-master named Fox, but very gentle,— the music becoming a shallow, rounded depression. Gentle, and an irritant almost hard to be conscious of. So that the simplest fact of his life, "specifically, a writer of music," was beginning to mean very little. And for years it was four o'clock,—not time which would have broken the hour and placed a statue of David in history, but an ornamental herb of that name,—with flowers that grow in Peru of a great variety of color. So that for years it was four o'clock and the same as bloom from 4 P.M. till the next morning. And since there was a memory of the hoofs of donkeys who had left him, there could now be the sum of three and one, and of twice two. The groups came in four units: a team of four horses, a playing card with four spots, quadrupled measures, a bedstead with four posts, a four-wheeler allowing passage in anyone of four directions. Golf for a foursome. In rows of townships, six miles in width, between two meridian lines, isolated groups composed of sympathetic individuals who had given free play to all the feelings and passions had reached the doldrums of Fourierism, but without success. In their hearths the phosphorescence of foxwood, and he was a bystander. They were foxtrotting, two couples and four friends, two friends and four couples, between a pace and a walk, between a pace and a walk. He could see the upper-leather of their shoes along the edges next the soles. They moved very gently and sadly.

He was in his own time, his fears too much aroused and prolonged, teased by repeated disappointments in the attainment of his object. If his notes could not extricate themselves from this complicated mass, they would be to his tactility like meeting at a point without further coincidence or intersection. If they did extricate themselves, they would, moving towards a definite shape, become capable of being apprehended, themselves their own existence in the plain of surrounding existence, tactility of materials become tangible. Lao-tse was working a Chinese puzzle consisting of a square cardboard cut by straight incisions into five triangles, a square and a lozenge—combining them into a variety of figures. It was a relief from ethics, an approach to the blue huckleberry. The tap-dancer was not a Chinaman. He was in a trench plunged to his neck in water, the fruit hanging above him. On a level with it a caterpillar tractor was pecking away at an acre of earth. Foolish, but there was the tap-dancer singing:

> Taps nailed upon the heel of shoe
> Make the water tantivy, tantivy, tantivy

Then he danced out very clearly and swiftly:

> My instep in the stirrup's
> tapadera

The tap-dancer was tapering towards the head, in a column of water growing conical, around, and containing, him. He heard a woman using a medicine composed of an ingredient of tansy say: One of the principal applications of tannic acid is in the preparation of writing-ink. He turned the tap-dance into a tango passing out in a diagonal shuffle.

Whirl, dip, and a swing! The duenna is a dragon! What is it, inflexible Draco, that is fabulous, has wings unlike a serpent, and is a monster! Come on! Come on! drag your brains! The Northern constellation? Guess again! A short, large-bored firearm of the 17th century or the soldier who carried it? That was before your time, what do you know about it? The small arboreal Asiatic lizard (genus *Draco!*) leaps aided by a parachute formed by lateral expansions of the skin supported by elongated and extensible hind ribs. What shall we say of the little flying lizards, what of the metamorphosis of the dragonfly, its four large wings and enormous eyes? Shall we call them with fourfold-thought of gentleness the devil's darning needle. The dragon is a duenna! The dragon has an inner paddle-shaft like a marine engine! The dragon is an excavator that draws the soil upward and away from the working-base thus clearing it. Scripturally, *tannim*, the meaning of which is uncertain. There went up a smoke out of his nostrils, and fire out of his mouth devoured: coals were kindled by it.—Wounds stink.— Caused men to ride over our heads. As smoke is driven away, so drive them away. (To the chief Musician, Psalms 18, 38, 66, 68!)

29
N.Y.

"At heaven's gate"   the larks: have
Read to date the nth reversion, "re" Marx

Of the mind's image   a hangar
A red crane—on the nearby wharves

In the spring-blue day—not working
But not out of languor

January the 29 , the 29th birthday
Falling on a Sunday

As planned there should be to-day
29 songs written over two years

And with, but without expected, pay

I have written down twenty-three
Leaving 5 and another page blank

To record a January without snow
For the delectation of the file and rank.

"Further than"—

Further than the wash-stand
three mountains in one bathroom
The mountains on the floor, sea-bed
rock, colored design; Five figures, chance
smudges, perhaps tar, in the mountains; Six
and Five figures in the waters under
and above them. Each figure
is an ordinate of which the axis
is a peak, The Whole Peak, from summit
thru base to inverted altitude, depth beneath
sea level. Only drying from the shower is
exploration possible, the chances
of world monopoly have been so carefully
seized that only on the other side of
one's bathroom nothing is foreign. Unless
charting the antarctic has something to do
with figures the heads of which are
just smudges away from the axis of abscissas
or one is merely exploring from a shower
expectant that today or tomorrow must
bring the new economic anatomization.

"Mantis"

Mantis! praying mantis! since your wings' leaves
And your terrified eyes, pins, bright, black and poor
Beg—"Look, take it up" (thoughts' torsion)! "save it!"
I who can't bear to look, cannot touch,—You—

You can—but no one sees you steadying lost
In the cars' drafts on the lit subway stone.

Praying mantis, what wind-up brought you, stone
On which you sometimes prop, prey among leaves
(Is it love's food your raised stomach prays?), lost
Here, stone holds only seats on which the poor
Ride, who rising from the news may trample you—
The shops' crowds a jam with no flies in it.

Even the newsboy who now sees knows it
No use, papers make money, makes stone, stone,
Banks, "it is harmless," he says moving on—You?
Where will he put *you?* There are no safe leaves
To put you back in here, here's news! too poor
Like all the separate poor to save the lost.

Don't light on my chest, mantis! do—you're lost,
Let the poor laugh at my fright, then see it:
My shame and theirs, you whom old Europe's poor
Call spectre, strawberry, by turns; a stone—
You point—they say—you lead lost children—leaves
Close in the paths men leave, saved, safe with you.

Killed by thorns (once men), who now will save you
Mantis? what male love bring a fly, be lost
Within your mouth, prophetess, harmless to leaves
And hands, faked flower,—the myth is: dead, bones, it
Was assembled, apes wing in wind: On stone,
Mantis, you will die, touch, beg, of the poor.

Android, loving beggar, dive to the poor
As your love would even without head to you,
Graze like machined wheels, green, from off this stone
And preying on each terrified chest, lost
Say, I am old as the globe, the moon, it
Is my old shoe, yours, be free as the leaves.

Fly, mantis, on the poor, arise like leaves
The armies of the poor, strength: stone on stone
And build the new world in your eyes, Save it!

"Mantis," An Interpretation

or Nomina sunt consequentia rerum,
names are sequent to the things named

Mantis! praying mantis! since your wings' leaves
  Incipit Vita Nova
  le parole   .   .   .
  almeno la loro sentenzia
the words . . .
at least their substance

at first were
"The mantis opened its body
It had been lost in the subway
It steadied against the drafts
It looked up—
Begging eyes—

It flew at my chest"

   —The ungainliness
   of the creature needs stating.

No one would be struck merely
By its ungainliness,
Having seen the thing happen.

Having seen the thing happen,
There would be no intention 'to write it up,'

But *all* that was happening,
The mantis itself only an incident, *compelling any writing*
The transitions were perforce omitted.

Thoughts'—two or three or five or
Six thoughts' reflection (pulse's witness) of what was happening
All immediate, not moved by any transition.

Feeling this, what should be the form
Which the ungainliness already suggested
Should take?

> —Description—lightly—ungainliness
> With a grace unrelated to its surroundings.

Grace there is perhaps
In the visual sense, not in the movement of
"eyes, pins, bright, black and poor."

Or considering more than the isolation
Of one wrenched line,

Consider:
"(thoughts' torsion)"
la battaglia delli diversi pensieri . . .
the battle of diverse thoughts—
The actual twisting
Of many and diverse thoughts

What form should *that* take?
> —The first words that came into mind
> "The mantis opened its body—"
> Which might deserve the trope:
> the feeling of the original which is a permanence
> ?

Or the feeling accompanying the first poor 27 words' inception
(the original which is a permanence
?),
That this thoughts' torsion
Is really a sestina
Carrying subconsciously
Many intellectual and sensual properties of the
        forgetting and remembering Head
One human's intuitive Head

                    Dante's rubric
                        Incipit
                    Surrealiste
                        Re-collection

A twisted shoe by a pen, an insect, lost,
"To the short day and the great sweep of shadow."

The sestina, then, the repeated end words
Of the lines' winding around themselves,
Since continuous in the Head, whatever has been read,
                        whatever is heard,
                            whatever is seen
Perhaps goes back cropping up again with
Inevitable recurrence again in the blood
Where the spaces of verse are not visual
But a movement,
With vision in the lines merely a movement.

What is most significant
Perhaps is that C—and S—and X—of the 19th century
Used the "form"—not the form but a Victorian
Stuffing like upholstery
For parlor polish,
And our time takes count against them
For their blindness and their (unintended?) cruel smugness.

Again: as an experiment, the sestina would be wicker-work—
As a force, one would lie to one's feelings not to use it

One feels in fact inevitably
About the coincidence of the mantis lost in the subway,
About the growing oppression of the poor—
Which is the situation most pertinent to us—,
With the fact of the sestina:
Which together fatally now crop up again
To twist themselves anew
To record not a sestina, post Dante,
Nor even a mantis.

Is the poem then, a sestina
Or not a sestina?

The word sestina has been
Taken out of the original title. It is no use (killing oneself?)

    —Our world will not stand it,
    the implications of a too regular form.

Hard to convince even one likely to show interest in the matter
That this regularity to which 'write it up' means not a damn

(Millet in a Dali canvas, Circe in E's Cantos)
Whatever seeming modelling after the event,
649 years, say, after Dante's first canzone,
If it came back immediately as the only
Form that will include the most pertinent subject of our day—
The poor—
Cannot mean merely implied comparison, unreality
Usually interpreted as falsity.

Too much time cannot be saved
Saying:
The mantis might have heaped up upon itself a
Grave of verse,
But the facts are not a symbol.

There is the difference between that
And a fact (the mantis in the subway)
And all the other facts the mantis sets going about it.

No human being wishes to become·
An insect for the sake of a symbol.

But the mantis *can start*
History etc.
The mantis situation remains its situation,
Enough worth if the emotions can equate it,

"I think" of the mantis
"I think" of other things—
The quotes set repulsion
Into movement.

Repulsion—
Since one, present, won't touch the mantis,
Will even touch the poor—

but carefully.

The mantis, then,
Is a small incident of one's physical vision
Which is the poor's helplessness
The poor's separateness
Bringing self-disgust.

The mantis is less ungainly than that.

There should be to-day no use for a description of it
Only for a "movement" emphasizing its use, since it's been around,

An accident in the twisting
Of many and diverse "thoughts"
i.e. nerves, glandular facilities, electrical cranial charges

For example—
line 1—entomology
line 9—biology
lines 10 and 11—the even rhythm of riding under-
                ground, and the sudden jolt are also
                of these nerves, glandular facilities,
                brain's charges
line 12—pun, fact, banality
lines 13 to 18—the economics of the very poor—the
                newsboy—unable to think beyond
                "subsistence still permits competi-
                tion," banking, *The Wisconsin Elkhorn
                Independent*—"Rags make paper,
                paper makes money, money makes
                banks, banks make loans, loans make
                poverty, poverty makes rags."

lines 22 to 24—Provence myth
lines 25 to 29—Melanesian self-extinction myth
line 33—airships
lines 35 and 36—creation myth (Melanesia), residue of
            it in our emotions no matter if fetched
            from the moon, as against l. 25 to 29.
and naturally the coda which is the
only thing that can sum up the
jumble of order in the lines weaving
"thoughts," pulsations, running commentary, one upon the other,
itself a jumble of order
as far as poetic
sequence is concerned:

            the mantis
            the poor's strength
            the new world.

39—"in your eyes"
            the original shock still persisting—

So that the invoked collective
Does not subdue the senses' awareness,
The longing for touch to an idea, or
To a use function of the material:
The original emotion remaining,
    like the collective,
Unprompted, real, as propaganda.

The voice exhorting, trusting what one hears
Will exhort others, is the imposed sensuality of an age
When both propaganda and sensuality are necessary against—
"—we have been left with nothing
just a few little unimportant ships
and barges" (British Admiralty even in 1920)

or jelly for the Pope

la mia nemica, madonna la pieta
my enemy, my lady pity,

36—"like leaves"
The Head remembering these words exactly in the way it
        remembers

la calcina pietra
the calcined stone.

But it remembers even more constantly
the poor
than
com'huom pietra sott' erba
as one should hide a stone in grass.

Nor is the coincidence
Of the last four lines
Symbolism,
But the simultaneous,
The diaphanous, historical
In one head.

                                        November 4, 1934
                                        New York

NOTE

The six blank pages intended by Song 29, written January
29th, 1933, were filled during 1933 and the early months of
1934 with songs 11, 23, 24, 26, 27, 28. Added to the original
collection their number is not included in, or for, the title of
the book, namely *55 Poems*. They are dedicated rather by
their subjects.

Anew
[1935–1944]

1

che di lor suona su nella tua vita

I walked out, before
"Break of day"
And saw
Four cabins in the hay.

Blue sealed glasses
Of preserves—four—
In the window-sash
In the yard on the bay.

Further:
The waters
At the ramp
Running away.

2

One lutenist played *look*; your thought was *drink:*
Then why like him pledge her to see?
Ben, all clocks stop in a house-party's eyes.
Music avoids impossibility.

If lonely she go with me from this room
We will look where lute notes dispose,
Whether from some rebellious dead, or still
One more earth where the marsh-marigold grows.

3

The green plant grows
Says your old man
But the white pot it is in
        Does not grow
The thorns are the roses'.

My old man's beard
Is older than your old man's,
And whatever song, the winds,
        And the snow,
Older than their prose is.

Went a lande a
Ship of Lusseboene but that lande
. . . All thinges is comune*
        As we know
As their suns' our sons' closes.

*Amerigo Vespucci

4

So sounds grass, and if it is sun or no sun
Sun on bur, or a noise in the ear's burr
A long sleep, and a full stillness.
It is Light. Circles

                star.

                Bur,
                Sum,
If they ask, it is you
Never with wilfulness,

A high fire fills a trench.
Sum, Egypt was a Sum, knows you as
Trench mortar and pyramids.

Sum, you are constructed, as of the tides, of your voice,
Water has this constancy, illness nothing,
By cheek bones
As of two as of many in the hills of Teruel

The guns of the loyal arms
Leaving the hands hanging from branches in snow,
River bottoms
And their shores where river bottoms were.

5

Ah spring, when with a thaw of blue
Sun in the street will she be as to-day?
Seaplane up to sky over sky
Avenues without empire an earth of May.

6

Anew, sun, to fire summer
leaves move toward the air
from the stems of the branches

       fire summer   fire summer

but for the people cheated
from the birds heard singing
thru four months on shore
toward the people in the waves

the green leaves that fill up the day
and those eaten away
—point-lace worked over a stem—
blow up on the trees of the cliff

on the top
the mill with the clock-tower
fires summer
           over a midsummer shore.

7

When the crickets
sound like fifty water-taps
forsaken at once

the inclemency
of the inhuman noises
is the earth's

with its roadways
over cabins in the forests

the sheets smell
of sweet milk

all the waters
of the world

we are going
to sleep to sleep

8

Has the sum
Twenty-five
Reduced the years
Of the live songs
To one-quarter
Of a century
Become cold mortar
Of a pyramid?
      Forget the number
Think of an entablature of snow
Engraved there 2 a bird-prow
Taking 5 in tow,
Then Ra look down
The figure shining thru the measure
Each song the midday
A sum of each year's leisure.

9

For you I have emptied the meaning
Leaving the song
Or would a god—a god of midday
Have been brought in by the neck
For foes to peck at

God the man is so overweening
He would prolong
A folly of thought see 2 as a bird
And what not that we rid day of
So that we may think in our time

Two birds tip on the guy wire
The green rained on
Is coppered by sunset, a treeling's
So black (together we hush a response) between
Its trunk and silk mesh of kirtle showed evening.

10

What are these songs
straining at sense—
you the consequence?

11

In the midst of things
One scotch and soda, and
Happy birthday! have you
Been walking in DICKEYVILLE
EIGHTEENTH CENTURY
DEVELOPMENT?
They turned
The walls of an old mill
There into a house.

VOICE OF THE HOUSE-DOOR
(Speaking after Catullus):
Sees all—
Time brings the guy with red eyebrows
In love with the Mrs. of this house
Who had her husband
After she had had his father.

(Pitying itself considerably)
Dazh the nizhest poem
I ever wrote exshepting
All the other nizher poems.

12

It's hard to see but think of a sea
Condensed into a speck.
And there are waves—
Frequencies of light,
Others that may be heard.
The one is one sea, the other a second.
There are electric stresses across condensers
That wear them down till they can stand no strain,
Are of no force and as unreclaimed
            as the bottom of the sea
Unless the space the stresses cross be air,
            that can be patched.
Large and small condensers,
Passing in the one instance frequencies
            that can be turned to sound,
In the other, alternations that escape,
So many waves of a speck of sea or what,
Or a graph the curve of a wave beyond all sound,
An open circuit where no action—
Like that of the retina made human by light—
Is recorded otherwise
Than having taken a desired path a little way
And tho infinitely a mote to be uncontained for
            ever.

This science is then like gathering flowers of the
        weed
One who works with me calls birdseed
That are tiny and many on one stem
They shed to the touch tho on a par
        with the large flower
That picked will find a vase.
I see many things at one time
        the harder the concepts get,
Or nothing
Which is a forever become me over forty years.
I am like another, and another, who has
        finished learning
And has just begun to learn.
If I turn pages back
A child may as well be staring with me
Wondering at the meaning
I turn to last
Perhaps.

13

A last cigarette
a companion

dark, spring's
green smells

and the work
is in mind

a love's
unclouding it

the spontaneous
idea

is not yet
called up

a green light
of the subway
entrance

to let spring ask
is the world

at the World's Fair
any more
than an action sings.

Science, too, posted
after all smells

carefully fostering
cadres

not grudging
time

patiently
"bothering."

14

"One oak fool box";—the pun
Retrieved from past days
Will soon be quicker than the thronged
Waiting room of the terminal in the dimout
In time of war,
When three trains leave within
      a minute of each other
For the same place:—
Here simmer the stray words of friends,
Guise of an agitation of electrical storms,
The accelerated impulse and emotion
              of events
Under the immense vault with
      extinguished bulbs,
In the granite columns

That derive unwieldy acanthus:—
The pun born of an oak file,
Of an aimless card index where there
                                    was peace:—
Dooley said:—and not so damned mute—
When the story of a great battle is written,
They'll print the killed,
The wounded, the missing,
And the seriously disturbed:—
As if some ancient head
Or its plaster cast,
Colorless water,
Said:—
If number, measure and weighing
Be taken away from any art,
That which remains will not be much:—
At least nothing like an
Appreciation of dawn
After the sixth day of work in one week:—
Or of snow melting from trees
If it falls with a sound of leaves.

15

No it was no dream of coming death,
Those you love will live long.
If light hurried my dream, I saw none:
Stepped from my bed and to the sill,
From a window looked down
On the river I knew set forth
To rise toward me—full after rain.
People watched, crowded the banks, thought
As with old words to a river:
(Whose waters seemed unwillingly
to glide like friends who linger while
they sever.) Soon, as expected!
A coffin launched like a ship's hull
Sped as from a curtain afire
Draped to the keystone of an arch
And—as at a burial at sea—

Sank. The displaced water rose,
Made the heart sound the coffin's grave,
Woke under the stream and in me
A set of furtive bells, muted
And jangling by rote "What does this say?
What loss will make the world different?
Are they gathered to further war?
What sorrow do you fear?
Ask, will you, is it here
Distrust is cast off, all
Cowardice dies. Eyes, looking out,
Without the good of intellect,
Rouse as you are used to:
It is the bad fallen away,
And the sorrow in the good.
You saw now for your book, *Anew.*"

16

I walk in the old street
to hear the beloved songs
afresh
this spring night.

Like the leaves—my loves wake—
not to be the same
or look tireless to the stars
and a ripped doorbell.

17
Guillaume de Machault (1300–1377)
Ballade: Plourès, dames

Cry for me, ladies, your servant
        Who said all he
May, I leave heart and intent,

Heart, my desire and thought, as your servant,
            To honor you
Whom God keep and augment.

            Dress yourselves in black for me,
            My heart fails my pale look (you see)
Death is all I see of this adventure
            If God and you
Do not take me for sure.

18

The bird that cries like a baby
Is the crow
Or a softer voice.
The turning spray of cypress
The seeming evergreen
With red falls of Virginia creeper
Nears the red of forsythia
That with the season lost its yellow.
Crickets keep filing away.
Forsythia named *Golden-rain* of parks
Appears wild in the country.
How like the west is the east
The sun setting sooner:
A tulip-tree by itself makes the autumnal east golden.
Before the clock was turned back an hour
This morning and it stopped saving daylight
A rescript was heard—
Caw—
Of the oldest Throne's baby,
"To enhance justice on earth
        and to make the world one household . . . "

Swimming in the creek
Water is colder and older.

19

And so till we have died
And grass with grass
Lie faceless as the grass

Grow sheathed with the grass
Between our spines a hollow
The stillest sense will pass
Or weighted cloud will follow.

20

The lines of this new song are nothing
But a tune making the nothing full
Stonelike become more hard than silent
The tune's image holding in the line.

21

Can a mote of sunlight defeat its purpose
When thought shows it to be deep or dark?

See sun, and think shadow.

22
Catullus viii

Miserable Catullus, stop being foolish
And admit it's over,
The sun shone on you those days
When your girl had you
When you gave it to her
          like nobody else ever will.
Everywhere together then, always at it
And you liked it and she can't say
                          she didn't

Yes, those days glowed.
Now she doesn't want it: why
            should you, washed out
Want to. Don't trail her,
Don't eat yourself up alive,
Show some spunk, stand up
                        and take it.
So long, girl. Catullus
                        can take it.
He won't bother you, he won't
                        be bothered:
But you'll be, nights.
What do you want to live for?
Whom will you see?
Who'll say you're pretty?
Who'll give it to you now?
Whose name will you have?
Kiss what guy? bite whose
                        lips?
Come on Catullus, you can
                        take it.

23

Gulls over a rotting hull,
Past a bridge their wings annul,
Are such fact the time must see:
Where no bridge spans war's decree,
Birds do, sea, ruin, burial.

24

The men in the kitchens
Their women in the foundries
The children in the wars
The old men at the boundaries.

25
for
Zadkine

It is a hard thing to say that when I first saw
La Prisonnière I wanted to run
And that I did, only that some birds then sang
In your courtyard, pursuing me
Over stone where you work in stone,
To come upon the prisoner in a field again.
Grass overgrowing ruins of the war
Over which she sprang, her head for other hours,
          above a wrecked column—
Like none that had ever been—
Nailed together maybe from broken curbs of wells,
          wood once now stone:
There, she was the Furies sometime called kind
Where the haunted stop on a ray of sun
Tho the bird still dreamed of pursues—
Any bird, that is, over a gravestone
Or a grave lacking one.
In the art of stone it is hard to set one's own
          seal upon the idea of stone,
And in a world from which most
          ideas have gone
To take the wreck of its idea
And make it stone
Raised up as a column
In which the prisoner is meant to be,
Over seas and fields and years,
Beside Daphne in the tree
And like a tree
But of stone to be seen in the sun,
Is harder.
There are almost no friends
But a few birds to tell what you have done.

26
1892–1941

To be moved comes of want, tho want be complete
as understanding. Cast, the statue rests, stopped:
a bronze—not "Grief"—the drapery should take in
body and head. The working eyes discarded.

Characterless lips, straight nose, sight, form no clue
(are none too great sculpture) to portrait or you.
At the seat of government, but a cab's jaunt
from the evergreens raised about the statue,

people count, climb the steps of the Capitol.
Shrubs, close to hands, that age at the visitor's
curved bench derive no clue from its smooth stone or
its simplicity or animal foot ends.

Nor shows the headstone back of the figure's seat
more than a blank emblem of two wreaths entwined,
bare in Eighteen Ninety Two, of our country.
Dark forearm not draped, hand modeled to the chin:

a lady of Nineteen Forty One met by
chance, asked where you could be found, took us three here,
left quickly, said, "The two of them lie there"

(I am one alive while two see here with me)

under the circle of purposeful gravel
feet must skirt or cross to come near the figure
over the gravel as on no other plot, in
"the cemetery known as Rock Creek": the name

gravel, those under. "One's instinct abhors time."

27
A madrigal for 3 voices

Hail the tree's meadow
Where the watch
Fees no property

    Where bread crumbs strike
      Red raked leaves
    Pigeons redden shadow
      Under red feet

              When pigeons greet
Workers meeting—
In the valley
      of the city—
Not a chimney's
      made of putty
And the lampposts
      are high
         high
            and white—or
         red, like
no property of
        night.

28

    The rains, the rains
    Toward spring pour thru
    The winter night
    And freeze to hail.

    Seasoned armies
    Tested in defeat
    Retreating now
    In that order

    They cannot yield,
    No more than weather

Of their hemisphere:
The rain that turns

To hail before
The thunderstorms,
The rains, the rains
Of spring call out.

29

Glad they were there
Falling away
Flying not to
Lose sight of it
Not going far
In angles out
Of ovals of
Dances filled up
The field the green
With light above
With the one hand
In the other.

30
A marriage song
for
Florence and Harry

Be happy you two
    Whose one aim
Makes the bride take
    The bridegroom's name.

As the birds on the hedge.
    Nor edge
Away in time
To ask how two
    May be
    Happy.

31

My nephew
And my new
Niece

Joy
On their wedding

From his mother
My sister
He never saw
And my mother
Her mother
Hers

      not to see

From my father
And his father

To the bride
Whatever she be

From the unconcerned
Dancers
Today

From the streets
From the walls
Of their house
Tomorrow

From where
He works

From the hills
From the sea

What if a thousand
Has been thrown
Away

Leaves of the fall
Gold

Blow away

Joy
On their wedding

Love tomorrow
Loved today

32

Even if love convey
His line, his tone,
We see him, alone,
Dissatisfied,
Tonight near yesterday.

See in his art
This tone the sun
And in this line his living eyes.
All was in place with him,
My valentine.

Even while on our green wall
His painting hangs
And makes new our will, oh
All artlessness cries:
"Sleep fast, I need the pillow!"

33

Drive, fast kisses,
no need to see
hands or eyelashes
a mouth at her ear
trees or leaves
night or the days.

34
The Letter of Poor Birds

The letter of poor birds
Is a wish or a song:
If we can be more, should we
On uninteresting land?
Today we saw hollows and low crests
The fallow, the arid, and the growing patch,
The yellow root of a red shrub
    make winter rosy
And cast such shadow on a white cottage.
The sparrows cram bread and drink. Do we
Drink more than water that flaws a drain?
You will believe they sang:
Jerry, Paul, Celia, Louis.

35
Or a valentine

What I did not say the other day to you for today
Is not unsaid because lost today with such thoughts
    in my head
That make one who looks up at the time say it has
    gone ahead.

36

       Strange
To reach that age,
              remember
    a tide
And full
    for a time
          be young.

37

The world autumn
Spiked seeds on undried branches
The tufted clouds
Where you look
So many falls for you
In the river
And where earth gives
Under each shoe

Past slate rock
You will see what soft blue is
With the sea
Such eyes as you have

38

    Belly Locks Shnooks Oakie
    When he awoke, he
    Scared all the spooks. He
    Was some oak, he
       Was.

One friend,
Red sealing wax, can say of us,
Their house—a woman and a man
Ate food and talked
Prolonged it but

To write, to sing:

White wax, dear face, Love,
Carry my child,—
Taper,—
Point us like any
Two plants.

40
Celia's birthday poem

No ache, love, 's the way to start the New Year,—
chant, then, "New Year" like "No ache" in your ear,
all the while I praise wind and love your face
above snow that melts over trees' space:
carol "No ache" like "New Year" between trees
that removed still share a few centuries.

41
After Charles Sedley

Not, Celia, that I look for rest
    In what I do or am;
In its own time this song addressed
    To you is not for them:

The hurrying world, our hastes have
    No part in you like me;
Faces stop showing what they crave
    In my attempt to see.

"All that in woman is adored"
      Grows my phrase, and your mind
Sings some hundreds of years to afford
      My cadence in kind.

And if your ears hear me I store
      It in our book *Anew*
Where we last who make Sedley—more
      Than he was perhaps—true.

42

You three:—my wife,
      And the one, whom like Dante,
      I call the chief of my friends,

And the one who still writes to me—
      This morning we are in the mess of history,
      That low crime, and like the devil in the book of *Job*

Having come back from going to and fro in the earth
      I will give the world all my hushed sources
      In this poem, (maybe the world wanted them)

I will be so frank everyone
      Will be sure I am hiding—a maniac—
      And no one will speak to me.

In any case, if it happens,
      I will not regret it one day
      That I am plain to the simplest.

But you three: my friend, my wife, and you,
      On whom my face and words weigh
      For whom pavement becomes too vague

To walk on because of me
      For whom the cracks in our plastered walls
      Cry out for me "I die! die!"

So that you want to shut your ears,
    Who begin to judge that something like my stars
    Weep on us the falls of black luck,

Who must be like myself and not pity me
    (I am, after all, of the people whose wisdom
    May die with them)

Who on top of the years cannot stand the thought
    That my tears too can be wet—
    I will ape a dead poet for you

And tell you of the little spirits of sight
    And the eyes, the beginning of love,
    And of the mouth which is its goal,

And of the appetite, he called heart
    And the reason, 'I call soul'.
    These words are better than I

And if I do die before you, as I have always
        wished,—
    Why, that's nothing new, I have always wished
        it,—
    They may speak to you, the equal

Of your own great anxiety
    As when I should have slept
    This morning and you were awake:

"He walks into door-jambs
    Never sees
    Where he goes

"He must do so many things
    In the morning, shower, brush,
    Clean his glasses a half dozen times,

"Pare his toe nails and cut his toes
    Remove the dirt from his finger nails
    After washing (for a clean person!)

"Shave with a dull blade, bolt breakfast,
    That after all night
    Reaching for his pocket flashlight,

"The kind they use in this war,
    To light up the face of his wrist watch
    'two-thirty'—after going

"To bed at two—
    'Two-fifteen'!
    'Three-fifteen, four o'clock,

" 'It is almost time to get up
    I haven't slept, I don't
    Think I will'—out loud!"

"Please"—"Okay! poet
    Did you ever get up
    Without aching

Without looking grouchy?
    You're not like your old father,
    Everyone looking at you would rather suffer instead of you."

I was thinking, shaving at the mirror,
    Will she write the music I cannot,
    Will he paint, probe, what I cannot

Will the other say the words that escape me?
    Will I, who must, write of my world's battle
    In which I have asked, and which I am not allowed,

To fight? Let your words be my testament.
    For I cannot believe we will not grow from them,
    When not needing even to conceive an aversion for anything

Despite the sage I will be dead
    And my thought in you for yet a while
    Wrapped in your words with a question—

Like that of Job's scourge—
    Do you know you are warmed in the earth
    By the south wind?

A beam of light, then, that you may still question.
    You three not divided, nor from me,
    In silence.

43
To my baby Paul

(After Guido)

Since we can't go back to Tuscany, Dinty,
We'll drink to you and Celia and to Jerry
And place her there who has never seen a
                  vineyard—
Drinking Chianti with us for the days
               when you will be growing.

NOTES

1
"che di lor suona su nella tua vita"
Continuing with Dante (limbo, THE INFERNO, IV, 77)

The comma in line 1 of this poem is meant as a pause
in the expectancy of the dream. Perhaps the capital B of
"Break," after the opening quotes of line 2, gives the feeling
of some unexpected person taking part in one's expected
activity: I was aware in the dream that I was writing a poem
and also aware of verses by others.

The word "bay" is what I could reconstruct later from the feeling of the action in the dream, as I moved from place to place, and should convey something of all the meanings of the word "bay": red-brown, the laurel, the laurel wreath, a bay horse, a deep bark or cry, a window-bay, a large space in a barn for storage as of hay or fodder, the state of being kept at a standstill, but more specifically two meanings that seemed to include all the others, they are, an arm of the sea and a recess of low land between hills.

The "glasses of preserves" were sealed with white wax.

The waters teemed like flood waters, but perhaps this is an afterthought. They were certainly *falls*, tons of them off the side, on a curve, and nearly on the level of the ramp, and the ramp seemed to be running away at the curve.

When I awoke the exact words of the poem I dreamt were lost, but those I wrote down still seemed to follow on the events of the dream. Later, that morning, Dante's "which sounds of them, up in that life of thine" seemed an appropriate explanation.

29
"Glad they were there"

> . . . e quelle anime liete
> si fero spere sopra fissi poli,
> fiammando forte a guisa di comete
>
> cosi quelle carole differente-
> mente danzando, della sua ricchezza
> mi si facean stimar, veloci e lente.

PARADISO, XXIV, 10–12, 16–18.

. . . it is a contradiction to say that a body is continually falling towards another and is at the same time continually flying away from it. The ellipse is a trajectory which, while allowing this contradiction to subsist, at the same time solves it.

. . . the bodily substance of the gold counts only as the embodiment of value . . . In its reality, therefore, it is exchange-value. Its use-value manifests itself solely in the ideal form, in the series of expressions of relative value, in which it enters into relation with the contraposing commodities as the complex of its real use forms. These antagonistic forms of commodities are the real forms in which the process of their exchange has its movement and its being.

DAS KAPITAL, Metamorphosis of Commodities

... general theory of electromagnetic field, and in which we constantly have in view the state of matter or the medium by which the field is occupied. While speaking of this state, I must immediately call your attention to the curious fact that, although we never lose sight of it, we need by no means go far in attempting to form an image of it and, in fact, we cannot say much about it.
... The second assumption relates to a magnetic field. Without thinking of those hidden rotations of which I have just spoken, we can define this by the so called *magnetic force*, i.e. the force acting on a pole of unit strength.
... It is not the motion of a single electron, nor the field produced by it, that can make itself felt in our experiments, in which we are always concerned with immense numbers of particles; only the resultant effects produced by them are perceptible to our senses.

Henrik Anton Lorentz
THEORY OF ELECTRONS, pp. 1, 2, 133

... luce e sta verde

Guido Cavalcanti, MADRIGALE

Some Time
[1940–1956]

Some time has gone
Since these were written:
The cause runs off—
A child's mitten.

But hear play the
Fingers of his hand
Celia perpends—
To understand.

Sequence 1944–6

1

I look at the pines on the hillside,
Alive,
And they not I who work
More or less absorbed
Have died.

2

But lose patience,
I lose patience.
Tied to song
Cannot speak.

We cross upon
One acre of music—
Asking
(So close who are cross)
Of acres and music:
Patience and time.

I am crazy about you

I feel
    sick.

3

Heart too human
To prefer the humane
That will not stop you
From beating again
And again

Wild

Thoughtful love
Crying, crying
Unreasoning child—

4

Having outlived self-offense
And that of my friends
I became brother to loneliness
And love the fact more than the word.

All that is human is
Alien and not alien.
All carefully chosen words
Are here—fairly shadows.

You have music to accord.
A child
At a remove from love
Holds leaves in my hand.

Where the world is headed
We do not say
As stars
Sun and surf

Flash in the sky. Were it said
Among twigs
"And then the world went
And then—"

Only our thoughts
Might seek it
In further woods.

5
(Flushing Meadows)

The flags in the water
Like grain that will not grow—
Out of the way
Out of the flow—

Silt and the sand
Where there is no harbor
Grow for the eye
That slows the hand.

A Song for the Year's End

1

Daughter of music
and her sweet son
so that none rule
the dew to his own hurt
with the year's last sigh
awake
the starry sky and bird.

2

I shall go back to my mother's grave after this war
Because there are those who'll still speak of loyalty
In the outskirts of Baltimore
Or wherever Jews are not the right sort of people,
And say to her one of the dead I speak to—
There are less Jews left in the world,
While they were killed

I did not see you in a dream to tell you,
And that I now have a wife and son.

Then I shall go and write of my country,
Have a job all my life
Seldom write with grace again, be part of the world,
See every man in forced labor,
Dawn only where suburbs are *restricted*
To people who take trains every morning,
Never the gentleness that can be,
The hope of the common man, the eyes that love leaves
Any shade, thought or thing that makes all man uncommon,

But always the depraved bark
Fight or work,
Dawn the red poster, the advertiser's cock crow,
Sunset a lack of wonder, the lone winged foot of Mercury in
    tie with a tire,
The fashion model
Her train stopped in the railroad cut
Looking up to a billboard of herself
As she goes home to her small son asleep,

So early and so late in the fortunes that followed
    me from my mother's grave
A lovely air follows her
And the dead President who is worth it:
'Dear death, like peace, I end not speaking,
The chitchat has died
And the last smile is unwilled
I am dead, I can't talk
To blossoms or spring in the world.'

3

    "Because he was crying
I like him most of all," says my son
"Because he was crying,"—the red fox
With three porcupine quills in his paw—

Who brings tears to the eyes,
    button nose against shambles,
Valentines all day, all night, tomorrow
The simplest the keyboard can play,
'Pony gay, on your way,' love's hair
With two gray, Papa Bear's Song
    new to renew,
'Who's been sitting in my chair?'

que j'ay dit devant

1

Day that passes,
Day that stays,
Day that passes
Other days'

Crow's-foot, sieges,
Tears, bare way,
A god's egis,
Catspaw spray.

2

Marry or don't
(If you wish)

Weigh the way in May
Given to brighter green
        Than that seen
Thru white curtain.

Love, weigh the way
Green, coat this May's green.
        No wish seen
Is uncertain.

Kiss the child's hard cheek.
Draw from a light green
                Away, seen
Thru white curtain.

It is the way the cheek
Shocks a bright green
                Makes it seen
Who is certain.

So That Even a Lover

1

Little wrists,
Is your content
My sight or hold,
Or your small air
That lights and trysts?

Red alder berry
Will singly break;
But you—how slight—do:
So that even
A lover exists.

2

Hello, little leaves,
Said not St. Francis
But my son in the spring,
Doing at two
(Neither really begged)
What it took the other—
He'd agree and laugh—
44 years to do.

Light

1

An instruction booklet on a certain effect
   in which
Mass becomes 0
Inertia approaches ∞

Light is critical
Time, immaterial
Distance, inside out.

2

   A house where every
               jigger
   is in place
   including
       a miniature outrigger

   such peace
   has no need
       to figure
   out who pulled
       the trigger.

3

Because Tarzan triumphs
See Tarzan the He-man
Go to sleep with boy in jungle corral
And chimpanzee, the best man, delouse
By the bed, hear that movie goer's giggle!
Clean,
Tarzan gives up his bed
        lush couch—
Thru with women: that girl

With her hair down in the world
Can take care of herself in his bed.

"Tarzan, boy's mother," he says slapping
The boy's rear, and
Reared by the jungle
He beats a man's breasts on his chest,
"He likes swimming," boy teases princess
"Swim with him!"
—Cupid, your thighs do play Cupid, boy,
She won't get far
If she wants thighs
Instead of high morals.
"She says you're an isolationist, Tarzan!"
Thwarted, the boy dawdles on the syllable *Tar:*
"A what! Boy?"
—Wait till he finds out!

You'll *have* to see how they do it
Tho evening prices go up quickly at noon.
"Nazi!" Tarzan says coyly
"Nazi," Tarzan says
And lures some celluloid to the lion's maw:
And all the earth's problems are solved.
You have seen
A rain of dried peas does not stick to a screen,
A non-stop reflector,
(Not the black sheet of a bed),
But an heroic
Which excretes and laughs.

4

These are not my sentiments,
Only sometimes does one feel that intimate.

                                    God, LL.D.,

            I want to resign
            You can have what's mine
            And what ain't mine,

I want to resign
What's mine ain't mine
What ain't mine is
            Thine,

                    SOS

P.S. I *want* to resign.

                5

Wire home:

It is always
Christmas
From the air
At night;

"So, He
        really
Lived?"

                6

An ornament of sentiment

He's a bit of red and gray—maybe green—rock
He's Pierrot the clown of Montauk.

He has no eyes, he don't talk—
He's Pierrot the clown of Montauk:

His cool existence admonishes
The cool yet bloody of the fishes.

Present him and walk down the beach—
He has no human tendency to squawk,
But! He's Pierrot the clown of Montauk.

Declaim his species like the clock:
Pierrot, Pierrot, Pierrot, PIERROT! —
He's Pierrot the clown of Montauk.

7

With a passion for a baby,
An age
Of zipper and plane.
The sun zips clouds, and
The wind's right back
And it won't rain!

Zip, zip, zip,
Eat quick, slo–o–ow.
The plane lands
And we meet:
The bull–itical guard, a–gain!

8

See:
My nose feels better in the air.

9

I was walking in the park
And a man came along
With his two tow-headed kids—
Boys: one 2, the other 3.
They may have been twins
They were so gentle together.
And he held out a small box camera:
"Mister, will you take our picture?"
I stopped. "Sorry,
But I don't know how,
If I did I would, gladly."
I believe they had been DP's in Germany.

"Well, look," the man said,
"You can see ourselves in the lens,
Then just press this down.
Wait! the sun must be behind."
He placed the kids
On either side of him:
Small, blue—papa, brown—small, blue.
Blue and brown showed in the lens,
The sun caught them in sky and clouds.
It was easier to
Handle his contraption
Than a song.
"The man took our picture, papa?"
"Yes, because we looked nice."
"Good-by." "Good-by." "Good-by."
. . . and good luck.
I have one print here.

10

A round

Isn't this a lovely field
In winter?

11

Who in snow
Has lain
Does not complain.

Whittle—
Whittle—
Wee Willie.

12
R.A.E.

Chance broke the jaw of this man
For no will could have done so
           To him.

Let him dead find such repose
That will dull the days
He is not in the sun—
Our ills and our plaints.

13

Why *daylight* saving?
At four in the morning, sun takes time
    to come up—under the horizon.

But once up
It's the sun.

Four hours sleep would be plenty
If today were enough to get up for
    and make coffee.

14

It never pours, it draws
On St. Valentine's—
An ocean
Secret with mines.

Magnetic hearts—
Moving shoeshines—
In the lines of force
Of St. Valentine's.

15

I'm a mosquito
May I bite your big toe?

Here's ten dollars

Use it
as you know.

I'm a fish
And I dance in your dish.

Here's ten dollars

Go and
say Hello, Hello,

You're Hey!

Happy
is
music!

The flute
The flute
The fluke

Michtam

*The lines are fallen unto me in pleasant places;
yea, I have a goodly heritage. Ps. 16*

1
Lese-Wiat, from Caul Gate

Caul Gate, Farewell, that hath me bound
And with an ointment laved my teethe

Until mine own voice tired, the sound
A quiet wasting summer's breath

Babylon his flood is stilled
Babel her tower doeth tie my tongue
In the willow path there it hath swilled
My spirit, His case, and young.

2
Romantic Portrait

Broad-bottomed Sealea
Whose potatoes are mealy—
Starched willy-nilly
His bosom grows hilly;

Whose head was cloudlike
Has become dowdlike:
His lips loose
Enough to suggest
The slack tongues
Of his shoes.

3
With a capital P

To the Gentlemen of the Press
With a capital P
A plea that in what sodden state he be
He will not veer nor keep his head on he

Attend him Star!
Especially in his motorcar.

Xenophanes

Water, cold, and sweet, and pure
And yellow loaves are near at hand,
Wine that makes a rosy hand
Fire in winter, the little pulse.

Eating a little pulse, who are you?
How old? The hands of all are clean.
Why first pour wine into the cup?
Water first and the wine above.

Better than the strength of horses,
I come back to my other words:
The hound, "Stop beating him, I said,
I knew him when I heard his voice."

For now the floor and cups are clean,
The aired earth at the feet is seen,
The rainbow, violet, red, pale green,
Men making merry should first hymn—

Non Ti Fidar

in opera poetry must be the obedient daughter
of music
Mozart

The hand a shade of moonlight on the pillow
And that a shadowed white would seem above or below
Their heads ear to ear, hearing water
Not like the word, the flickflack of the eye opening on it
With what happiness
Where the word is the obedient daughter of music
And Don Giovanni's shapely seat and heart live in hell
Lovable as its fire
As all loves that breathe and kiss
Simply by life
Rocking to sleep and flame:

So frail is judgment
It must light up, an overseer
With some truckling in hell,
A song that lovers' heads
Ear to, and on ear foretell.

Chloride of Lime and Charcoal

I

1

There when the water was not potable
Because of too many microbes
The health officer proposed
Hanging a bag
With a mixture of chloride of lime and charcoal
Ten feet down in,
To purify the well.

2

Zinnias you look so much like Gentiles
Born among butcher furniture
Who lived Easter and Christmas
Whose fathers died without wills
And left land to divide
    among they forget
Which spinsters and
The son a saint they must have called him
    soft in the head
To whose salt marsh—it happens I like
    cattails—Jewish I am mortgaged.

Almost prize flowers, large—
I am taken aback by a difference
As by his small wife's girth
While the rest of her sweetness suffers arthritis
Whom I greet in the way
My own wife hurried to arrange you in our coffee pot

The first vase at hand
A something to give
One whose cares should be
A velvet painting of zinnias
But not her sons running off
     she might think not to learn.

As your rose, pink, yellow, and orange
Are mixed in the melting pot
That the kindness of our mortgagers
Created with you at leaving you at our door
And tho your givers begin to shake hands with my kind
Do the snobs, salvagers of culture and religion dare suspect
We are saved, formally, by green?

So: these are your lancet leaves, tubular stems
Stopped in the lotus or artichoke of your sepals
Of Egypt.

3

How sweet is the sun, is the sun
How sweet is the sun
With the birds, with the summer months
     the notes of a run
How sweet, sweet is the sun.

You ask what I can do—
My name is Jackie
I am Jack-of-all-trades:
Homer—the carpenter—
Did you write that book?
Is your fir squared
     and its end true?

How sweet is the sun, is the sun
How sweet is the sun
With the birds, with the summer months
     the notes of a run
How sweet, sweet is the sun.

II

Homer's Argos hearing
Handel's Largo as
The car goes

Or

The dog in the third story
Brownstone window looks
Down into the street
Left and right
Much like his master
Distracted,
To see
What is going
On in the world.

Is the skyline still there
Are the buildings
A new bridge
Or the new ramp?
Philosophy moves
Faster than sound
To what purpose?

Until lights hang—
As if—from the skyscrapers—
Down a mist?

Indian summer, november first,
Evening of cantilevers of finance
Death (is?) the common share
Of the loved.

Stone struck
By hanging jewels
And hung off iron.

Are they coming home, master?

Ah, my craft, it is as Homer says:
"A soothsayer, a doctor, a singer
and a craftsman is sure of welcome
where he goes." Never
have I seen anything like you,
man or woman.
                I wonder looking at you.
Well, in Delos
once I saw something like you,
a young palm sprung at Apollo's altar,
I've been even that far—along
with others and their raft of trouble.
Seeing that sapling I was stunned
for no other tree like it grows out of the earth.
And yet I wonder and am stunned—
you might be that girl—
at the thought of touching your knees.

Reading and Talking

Cauliflower-eared Spartan
Who go about
Your cestus bound to the hand
What are you hiding
The cestus girdle
Of Aphrodite
That sends love on the wind
Has not lifted?
What is the hurdle—
That you rule the world
By such wisdom?

And Plato said, not
Much better
Than a few things:
'Nor when love
Is disinterested

Is there any disgrace
In being deceived.
All creation into being
Is poetry or making.
But that
Made with music
Is named poetry
The same holds
Of love, only desire
Of good
Is the fire and light
Power of love.

They drawn towards
Love by the path of money-making,
Gymnastics, or philosophy,
Are not named lovers.
The simple truth is
That men love the good.

Would you like
The truth about love
In any order
That comes
Into my mind
At the time?'

Make music, Socrates,
The dream bids
Like the runner
Bid by eyes that see:
To run as he is
Already running.

And Plato forgot to keep still
Building
A so-called good-for-all
With a cestus.

But I take it
   Too
He said—
Talk is a form of love
Let us talk.

The voice that first startled
    bodies
After they fail continues
To startle minds with abstractions
That hearts may pound again—
To a grammar
Aping a carved throw stick
Reindeer horn,
Tusks,
Lines, graves of lions,
The blood of old cave drawing

With new artifacts
Startling
A modern cave

      (Present?)

As a coda begins—
   A simple—

   That year's
   poem
   will be
   better

   if tears
   show him
   to the
   letter.

"As to How Much"

Of the right way
That branches may be
Described—
Laden with snow—
What proscribed
A limit long ago?

We do not know
Of any we see—
Inscribed
Here bark is next snow.
Love is so. Thrived.
And we do not know. No.

As to how much
Such love may be
Ascribed
To bark or snow
You proscribed
Some music long ago.

George Washington

Is it possible
Some Virginian
Laughing in
Snow's gust
Eye on beast, covert
At land
So virgin
Saw there
A father
Who could not lie.

Framed him and goat:
Who would not lie,
Nor wood, a cherry—
And chopped the

Tree down:
So people
Make blue sky,
Wig and dust white,
And covert cloth
For the first
In the hearts of—

Chopped the
Cherry tree
Down—
And chopped—
It is possible.

And Without

And without
Spring it is spring why
Is it death here grass somewhere
As dead as lonely walks
As living has less thought that is
The spring.

Spring it is spring why
Is it death grass somewhere
As dead as walks
As living has less thought that is
A spring. And without.

Perch Less

Perch less, bird
Fly on the
Leaves
Be heard
Spatter drops
So nothing is
But light
So light so well
Foolishness is joy.

Butt age, boy
Have it not tell
You, *swift but*
Is nothing so
Light it drops—
From such high
Slurred notes
Bow-hair dares bird:
So light so well
Foolishness is joy.

Air

How my city has grown!
Privet close at the window,
We have seen
New stone at the old thrown down,

Springs coiled; iron rib, spade
The excavation for the tunnel
Over which
The approaches meet at grade.

For all their metal we are not alone—
Hedge and human
As it were sun winds met on Sunday
High up and in a street of stone.

This Egypt, a downtown never to go
But, under bridge a river, to harbor
With a thought
Of ashlar to arbor.

My father praying at my mother's grave
Heard his father's song
Love and book
Not their dust where we don't pray.

We are so much alive, child, were
All his city's old graves to go
Out of sight, its harbor
Would carry his old air.

Pamphylian

Whole night in form the whorl on earth
Of Er Pamphylian by birth
Whom Plato broad forehead and throat
Held as eight sirens hymned one note.

Chains of heaven let down their waves
Three voices sound here one tone craves.
These? The daughters', of necessity.
But this thing then that has plenty

Understands together fails not
Of future nor frees its past thought
And so mighty that all be right
To touch in the middle of light

Pleasance and presence of trace
A feathering moving a face
Who are mine having nothing to save
For your grace such it cannot but have.

To My Valentines

From one to two
is one step up
and one and two
spell three
and we agree
three is the sum
                a run
of two and one.

On Valentine's Day
to
Friends

The hearts I lift out of snow
    So few,
The one, two or three, say few
    Friends who
Eye a heart, wish well what
    I do,
Befriend its festival
    When to
Persist I sing of Celia and
    Of Paul
To R'lene and Edward, Lorine,
    Or all—
Tags, René—that can with a red heart,
    Valentine,
Brush a white-velvet heart in snow
    falling deep to speak
    Be mine.

Alba (1952)

In sleep where all that's past goes on—
A dawn loves more than sleep.
Clear as leaves of spring.

Loves no less, wintering,
Greener than summer goes—
A sleep gainsays the dawn.

Old

    'More do I love cold
    than do I hate warm.'
    If what the child hear
    sound old, neither does
    cold hate warm.

The more if less love
may do hate out
of its charm.

Spook's Sabbath, Five Bowings

I
spiccato

There was the mechanicalism
of the ice cream scooper,
the Malayan violinist
more expressive than any Caucasian
as he melted into his Schumann
so for his part hard objects
became the buttocks of the heart.

II
martelé

No sins or
Faux pas
Disturb a *repas*
À l'hôtel
The
Hotel Windsor.

Day begins or
Ends
The knee bends
To the rustle
Of cards
At the Windsor.

Never a fiesta—
A siesta
Has emptied
All the chairs

Of sins or
Faux pas
At the Windsor.

III
grand détaché

The night
the skunk
stank up
Adirondack
"the village beautiful"
Celia dreamt
of renting
outhouses
under
compunction
and beneath
contempt
while Louis
with usual
curiosity
as to *real*
estate
hung round
to look into
all, and
at last
two
to see
which
was
the better
for the
violinists'
trills
above
around
about—
brooked by

an inexorable Teacher
swayed
to the
Rode.

IV
collé

When *The Mill*
the artists colony
burnt down
we rushed
to its
end of town
to ask
"How did it happen?
Was anybody hurt?"
"No, the tank blew up
on my competitor—
my best friend—
there was no stopcock
and in this heat the oil—"
(sculptors had saved some
underwear
upon the pines)
said George, fifteen,
with teeth,
crew cut black hair,
in his "father's truck"—
stopping on a rival
call.

V
staccato

Said Susan, dear Susan
"I could faint
But I'll paint,
My relations

Who bought a cottáge here
Are all
Drinking potage."

Then Eva the diva
Sang over-all, ah
What is
The matter?
Poor good people yet so strange
I would say
With Shakespeare
They make *mows*
For *hellos*. Not so?
An effervescence makes them retreat,
Hello, a mew, never stop, go—
They pass out
On the street
I travel everywhere,
Italy—I make friends
With whole villages
All are happy, all live,
Live!
I live here too
Never mind,
I sing, I eat, I dress
And grow fatter.

"All Wise"

Footprint and eye fringe
Shake off snow—
All wise
Flinging.

Pupil and fingers
Draw the bow—
All wise
Singing.

Heartbeat and feathers
Sow birds so—
All wise
Ringing.

For
Selma Gubin's
Umbrellas

Reality is and is
not commonage,
painting
is paint—

three headless
coats under
three
umbrellas

two yellow
and one blue,
a play as on
nightshade or eggplant,

worn like each coat
to open differently
on tubby figures
walking in shoes

red hands
around red handles
the red
holds grasp

where those other
colors
distributed
by it

are here for
a yellow splint
T'd by a shorter
slanting

that's post
hanging
a lamp
but a small

white
circle
out of
moon

a light
umbrella-wise
a way
distributed—

seen
as when
color first
made shape

by color
dividing
joining
color

until what
period
comment
followed

rain is wet
wind hugs cold
green is a patch
snow melts

into slush
in one
age
of the street

on which
as paint
are there
or are there not

three Chinese
in one spot
who don't
meet

sunlight is
on the ground
storm is in
the sky

and an after,
before, of time
but a no time
in things

so shared
no word attacks
and never
loses.

The Judge and the Bird

The house was Dutch
in style
of which there is—
not much.

Corbie gable,
corbel
derived
from the raven

for the reader
of a herbal
under the high
window
of colored panes

shadowing
rainbows
on
oak floor.

The old judge
dead now
lived to bring up
his trees

was well-read
on his herbs,
and his poets
in fine bindings.

Winter's gone
spring has come
and summer's here
his son rents to us.

We breakfast
facing a mountain:

a yellow—wild!
a yellow leaf—
not fall's
the yellow leaf a thought—
is yellow bird.

Casual
the wild canary's South
shows north, songless,
yellow on
pennywort

yellow near myrtle
upon moss
next my lady's-thumb-grass.

Its song its yellow says
    that stills—
the mouth
tastes pine and raspberry
digitalis and wild rose

that the tongue which may sing
be casual—
as Dutch leaf is cheap,
a gold—

as old as the Dutch style
as such of a judge
a wild South brings yellow
today—

singing of it
in crossing the brook
he deliciously called
The Bouquet.

All of December
Toward New Year's

1

Not the branches
half in shadow

But the length
of each branch

Half in shadow

As if it had snowed
on each upper half

2

A tired—much less—an old
man does not talk of justice
—much less an old man
having nothing, nothing like
content

3

A WORLD ATLAS in a globe base:
Who turned the print to us?
We don't need to read it.

Turn it to the toile
That hangs on the wall,
The hand-blocked figures
Such blue shades
Should read it
And come to life,
The young sun.

The young son:
"If it's turned
from us, we
are the shades."

H.T.

Being driven after the hearse thru suburbs—
    the dead man who had been good
    and by a coincidence my father-in-law,
I sped by shop signs:

Handel, Butcher, Shelley, Plumber
a beautiful day, blue wintry sky
such is this world.

SONGS OF DEGREES

1
With
a Valentine
(the 12 February)

Hear, her
Clear
Mirror,
Care
His error.
In her
Care
Is clear.

2
With a Valentine
(the 14 February)

Hear her
(Clear mirror)
Care.
His error.
In her care—
Is clear.

Hear, her
Clear
Mirror,
Care
His error.
In her,
Care
Is clear.

Hear her
Clear mirror
Care his error
In her care
Is clear

Hear
Her
Clear
Mirror
Care
His
Error in
Her
Care
Is clear

Hear
Her
Clear,
Mirror,
Care
His
Error in
Her—
Care
Is
Clear.

3
'Nor did the prophet'*

The birds are our friends—
    Jannequin's,
    The sun's.
The man is our friend?
Our friend.

I know why David moves me,
"The worst bastard of them all"
Never chartered nor coddled his ground.

The sound in the Temple built after exile
Is never worth the sound
At the earth where no temple stood
And on which no law of exile can fall.

Blood flows; not hateful good,
Not this measure is blood.
Crabbed and lovely both is root.
What is never imposes.

The tree's good of the field of Machpelah
As of Persia or of Mytilene.
Who comes as Cyrus proclaims,
Rocks later with Artaxerxes,

For all Darius gives—
Rends coat, plucks hair of his head
                    and his beard
Sits down astonished

And does not stop from drinking water
As blood is shed—
Does not see morning without a cloud
Upon tender grass after rain.

On this earth
We will not—nor did the prophet much—
                            mention
David.

The birds sing:
The man is our friend,
Our friend.

*Ezra 1–6; I Chr. 6.31, 15.16; II Sam. 23.4; Gen. 23

4
Happiest February

Many more happy Valentines.
How many?
As the last
          makes no sense.
As many as many.
As more rolls out the vines
Which shade green in the snow
Of a cold fourteenth
Of their happiest February.

5
William
Carlos
Williams

alive!

thinking of
Billy

The kid
shoots
to
kill,

But to
the expanse
of his
mind

who heard
that word
before,

scape
of a
letter

soars
with the
rest of
the letter

gulled by
the kid's
self-sacrifice:

reach
C
a cove—
call it
Carlos:

smell W
double U
two W's,
ravine and
runnel:

these
sink
high

in
high
fog

which
as
it
lifts,

the other
world
is
there:

the sight
moves—

open—

soothes

smoothes
over

the
same word

that
may have,
to touch,

two faces—
the heart
sees into—
of one
sound:

the
kid
's torn,
shot

so quickly
it sounds
water:

purls

a
high
voice

as with
a lien
on
the sky

that becomes

low now
frankly

water—

called also—

softly—

a kill.

6
A wish

Looking down at the water
three blocks away at Clark Street
if but once a day,
    my valentines,
but day after day,
my mind going to work
with eyes on the water
tries me with a prayer,
    my sweet,
that my wish wear our look
well, care for our days:
    to long life!
So the song be for good
and that time a new's written
the water flow on,
as there now, it be a completion
to wharves below, a street
away. A way—

a good sprag memory
so the boy profits lively.
It would make sense. As if there now
that time brightens a page—
stretched as by Providence—
of a mind that
in the Latin of Parson Evans—

telling the boy the vocative
Remember, William, is 'caret'—
Shakespeare went before
to touch Bach who taught
his choir boys Latin
in the while
proved by the fugue

Look, where his master comes;
'tis a playing-day,
I see.

See I, day-playing
a 'tis;
comes master his
where,
Look.

7
March first

Remarkably all this March first
Would-be, small leaves are making a hell
                                    of a noise,
Littlest children fight with their fathers,
The mothers are distracted or
                        stark mad
Rehearsing with them—
Tiniest green and teemingest teen—
        Reciting
"We are the generations of leaves."

The Guests

In the mountains
the finches

are
four chairs

arranged
catty-corner

before the window
on whose sill

tomatoes ripen

from above
on the
chimney
piece
the clock

ticks
down

at the door
the lawn
rolls
to the road

lined
one side by

rock wall
the space
in it
the gate to
the garden

a side post of
goldenglow
a side post of
apple tree

the garden
for what

came
to the table

as herb
or green

or vine

a mown
tract then rolled

to the two-hundred
year pines
the brambles
the woods
the sometime dry brook

brimming for once
with
wished-for
rains

and the range's
rim rose

five thousand feet

the view
from the window

two chairs
for the occupants

two chairs
standing
for the ever-returning
guests

Claims

Ferdinand
Pericles

a poet wrote a long story with the first name
his title, and without thought that a thought
had carried over went on to the second for
a title, certain the name made Shakespeare's song
To sing a song that old was sung, From ashes—
Antioch's. Both names it occurred to him,
glad ten years with the second, mean *risking life*.
To pronounce the first letter of the first
the lower lip's bit by the upper row
of teeth, while the upper lip furls, the breath
as if held about the palpable heart;
to announce the first letter of the second
both lips persist passing teeth and the heart's breadth.
After ten years he thought thought is that risk
whose claim claims claim, *Ferdinand* stakes *Pericles*
as the breath blown follows a breath drawn in—
as the body has the thought it will live out
as what is after begins what was about.

The Laws Can Say

for P.Z.

We may not always rate
An Idaho potato—
A satisfying meal
Holds more than broken Plato.

If undersigned
Has wonder signed
It is not *prior to,*
Neither/nor, nor *and/or*

Under the law's fedora.
The best *and/or* we sing
Who hold is always
In Andorra.

Shang Cup

From a libation cup
of bronze
which stands

on a thought
its three feet are man—

so any pair of two
make wonder, sign

a writing of that stance
seen from all planes

as the base
cradling the cup

with half-circle
of an ancient ear
the handle—

a turtle dove
sings in jade
nests part of the lid

closed on the lip

but its beak and wings
raised to heaven

this way
the eye of it
looks up

singing
come sip
I drink.

An Incident

leaning on my left hand
holding a cigarette
too close to the ear
shocked
I heard its ashes
crackle
as if a bonfire
lit up
yesterday—
and equally
forgetful
today.

The Record

Some years before we were married Celia gave me a record-
ing of the orchestral music of *Eine kleine Nachtmusik* for a
birthday present, the quartet music of which our son Paul
would perform the first violin part on her birthday, Jan. 21,
1956, at a public concert celebrating the 200 anniversary of
Mozart's birth 6 days later.

Our valentine the heart proposed by three,
Our vanity that talks and cannot see
As it fell out—the girl who loved brought me
The record we played for ourselves years way
Before our son bowed it on your birthday,
   Against fall-out,
   Never to fall out—
Delight, Amadeus, to light
The music of a little night.

Barely and widely
[1956–1958]

Barely
and
widely

love

they say—
        in these words—

of Paul
      "barely
            twelve"

and of me
        "widely
           published

        throughout
                a long
                    career"

    So unknown

Celia
      you are the peer-
          ess of this
               song

making the news notes
sing
    as there

our music is called—
    smiling
        "Make sure

call your next book—
              Barely and
                            widely"

dear.

1

This is after all vacation. All that
matters is, all that matters—neither am
I, intent on poems, desirous of hearing
all these violin and piano sonatas
every morning for over two weeks and—
tired you would rather not—
as for the young violinist who'ld gallivant
rather than work fingers for stops,
fingers for keys—
yet really not. He will say: *all that* matters.
The music comes from another time
and sings it is *so,*
but it *may we* be believed,
know fingers for keeps,
creditably conceive the changes of times
retained in different pieces of music
as a *matter* of us so *they* are believed:
Beethoven's second and fifth violin and piano
sonatas have come to the measure
of two different rooms,
two instruments affecting a third creature
so young he exists in all rooms;
from low string sounds hautboys, such
as treasure today mere oboes, and now
hunting horns, and again strings are themselves
or flutes in the higher positions,
and from piano keys,
which some fiddlers scorn,
cellos, and from
the G string—airs, airs.
All who matter have come
without effacing *ever,*

so easily said, as unlacing
what is
from what was
those who have just got up
may lead or be led back to bed
having contemplated without template to
flower so.

2

You who were made for this music
or how else does it say you,
move thru your fingers, or your bow arm, lead
to this glory: God has—God's—
but one's deepest conviction—
your art, its use—you, happy,
by rote, by heart. Is thought?
What was broken was sense
but is happy again almost seen,
the first trembling of a string a worth
whose immortal ground drops so often
you plait viable strands for your use.
Or so pride loving itself looks
to more fortunate glory, with a power
apart from the trembling sense
only glory restores.

3

The green leaf that will outlast the winter
because sheltered in the open:
the wall, transverse, and diagonal ribs
of the privet that pocket air
around the leaf inside them
and cover but with walls of wind:
it happens wind colors like glass shelter,
as the light's aire from a vault
which has a knob of sun.

4
A Valentine

This
is
not
more
snow
to
fall

but
a
gust
of
the
softest—
bending

down
the
wood
of
gardens'
branches
into

a
girls
and
boys
pastoral,
old

years
not
to
wink
looks,
middle

life
to
chase,
it's
musical

5
The Heights

The sun's white in the high fog
that a thin mist at the eyes
shows to this harbor makes see white
and extends white with wide gray of
water as into some foreign public square—
one yacht sail, few dark screws of smoke
float a deceptively unflowing threshold
for the grayed walls on the other
shore: then like quick speech the pearled cartoon
of skyline, of windows curiously
close to pavement here, what is heights
very near under at this stage.

6

Send regards to Ida the bitch
whose hate's unforgiving,
why not send regards?
There are trees' roots, branchtops
      —as is
one who can take his own life
      and be quit
except he might hurt—as
      he imagines
here he's gone—
a person, two; if not the sun.

7
Stratford-on-Avon

1957

The Midlands' *a* is mostly an *i*
Said like *eye*—
"We don't fancy Shixespeare here—
People come from all over the world
To see the birthplace and the grave—
But we have a picture house we go to;
The top of the station is the way
        to Anne Hathaway's cottage at Shottery,
Mary Arden's house is at Wilmcote, 4 miles
        from Henley Street."
"You've a factory here,
Stratford's become industrial?"
"Not really, those are our gas works
        you see at the bottom."
"You need gas to cook with at that, don't
        you?"
And his remains that two Americans
        and their growing son came to see
Might be thought loving
Those works too—
Tho not so much as the mother
        guiding with her baby in the pram
The three ran across again later,
        several times,
As they strolled thru the town.

She had green eyes—
No tall perch, Helena,
Of the Bard's or Swan's
                midsummer dream,
Rather small Hermia
        with whom tall Helena pleaded,
We, Hermia
Have with our neelds created both one flower,
Both on one sampler, sitting on one cushion,

Both warbling of one song, both in one key—
*   we grew together,*
*   a double cherry, seeming parted.*
Not tall personage, rather
Hermia—who as
The course of true love never did run smooth,
Guessed love's hell is
O hell! to choose love by another's eye,
Taught *trial patience*
*   a customary cross*

        Until
        Theseus judged:
No doubt they rose up early to observe
*   the rite of May*
Good morrow, friends. Saint Valentine is past:
Begin those wood-birds but to couple now?

Maybe as do all the flowers Shakespeare
        remembered
Today planted in the garden
Back of the Birthplace

Good friend for Jesus sake forbeare
The slab might be thought to pray
        for itself
Stone in the chancel stone
Looked on by the full-blown polychrome
        bust
Which such as it is might also not seem
To fancy Shakespeare here—

Anne Hathaway's burden—

And the new Queen's,
She dedicated
A rose tree
Altogether
Too wiry to see;

167

Or the dark
Young man's
With the Midland *ai*
Forelock,
And a girl on his arm,
Teasing:
"The one blotch
On the Shakespeare arms
In Stratford
Is the Memorial Theatre
A woman planned"
As the family of three
Can no longer
Live by thinking
Has one smile,
"That may not be bad
If it turns out well."

8

This year
that Valentine is
late—

not that the
view
distracts,

on Washington's Birthday
the cold
is

lonely
the Flag too
over Governors Island

between the Statue
of Liberty
and

the cruiser
still
in midwater between

the copings of
two
buildings (as

an island in
itself
towards

the hills of
Staten
Island)

since
Valentine's Day—anchored
for the

Picture Post Card
of the crescent
of

his evening
and the red sky
and

the blue
and
for this once

forever,
the
white

star
that is
you.

9
Ashtray

The baited
bear
on
the ashtray

shows more
flare
than the
tramp

in his whip
tho
perhaps
enough's

there
to
give them
heart.

10
Another Ashtray

Three
crimson
mongrels
bait

the whip
in a boot
on a
leg.

11
Head Lines

A San Francisco chronicle.
The voice of the West.

Paternity: 2 men say
They want boy.

'I'm the father,'
Both men say.

Krushchev
won't debate
satellites.

12
4 Other Countries

Merry, La Belle
    antichi, tilling—
of pastime and
    good company:

Tea in England
    as much as you eat
it saves face
    the fill hole's petite—

Luggage, the
    tour complete
the buttocks
    wet—

On the way to
    Tours, the russet
cow, bordering
    the river

La Gloire in the black
          flags of the valley
of the
          Loire—

A lavender plough
          in Windermere
the French blue
          door

Of a gray
          stone
house in
          Angers

Walled farms
          little lanes
of entry, orange-
          red roofs

A period farm
          cowboy on
a live green
          rivulet

Longs
          for ranches
cultivated
          plains

A horse opera
          of Indians
to end with
          the train's past.

On the route
          to Poitiers
a garden of
          purple and red

As only the French
        can plant
in front of
        an arcade of poplars'

Arc de triomphe
        infusing all
madeleine memories
        of the Ouest.

Bedlam
        Paris
Roman
        London—

Where stop
        who have spoken to
old friends
        for the

First time
        years
sing to
        speak

There is no
        quiet in the
world—a
        wedding-

Cake Tower of
        Babel
that is
        Nice—

Nor drive
        chasing
shape
        in rock

Color
    of Lascaux
bones,
    Eyzies.

The birds of
    Périgueux
sing back Gaul
    Roman and Jew

Middle Ages slum
    merde at St. Front
pendentive
    of Istanbul

Arcades, basilicas,
    chevets, the Tower
of Vésone
    in honesty

Warning
    Stay away
the wall
    crumbles—

The
    park's
a garden
    landscaped with

A butterfly
    of flowers'
hanging spread
    on ground,

Red rose fall
    in the small
arena's ruin
    red briar

Song in
     marbles of
Bertran de Born
     and Girault de Borneil.

This hush that
     the bard
is writing
     again

The vowels
     abide
in consonants
     like

Souls
     in
bodies—
     paradise is his

Hand,
     paradise
our
     speech;

To perfect
     makes
practice,
     a ray of

Sun
     he spoke
too soon,
     as on the

Legendary
     map
the
     criminal

Dropping
　　always in
monk's garb
　　into the

Grot
　　lower
than the
　　rise

He
　　first
began,
　　as a hole

In a head
　　St. Michael
made
　　in a bishop

Sent
　　to sit
for an
　　eternity

To look thru
　　one window
of a
　　Merveille

Not with eyes
　　but after
he had died
　　and built

Up to the mount
　　where the Druids
in white surplice
　　sacrificed—

Red drops
        blinking
to the Three Kings
        rubies—

Master
        Aristotle's eternal
whiteness of
        a day.

Benedictine
        initial—
golden green
        serving

Pontorson
        with croissant
on breakfast
        gingham

A
        bottle of
liqueur
        Michelaine

A tourist
        forgot in
the gap
        of a removed stone

Under an
        arch of
a
        stairway

Of the
        Perilous
Castle,
        under

Which
    endless wind
stirring
    reflections

Of clouds
    reaches water
on an Elysium
    of sand—

Yellow,
    pearl,
shadow,
    gloss-

Black—
    in one's
youth
    old women

Begged in
    the street
all the way to
    the archangel

Saint Cecelia
    who cannot praise
them
    smiles

They have
    turned young
again in shops
    on sales

Of fake
    Quimper,
Durham's
    more solid

With Bede's tomb,
    Chartres'
two towers
    as once

Measure
    Leoninus
to
    Josquin.

Merry
    La Belle are
England
    France

Short of
    a month
of pastime
    blossoms

The wish
    that of
good company
    there be

No end
    sped around
wall
    of rock

Over
    the Middle
Sea
    to where—

He
    was at
via Marsala 12
    an era gone

179

Now known
    of no one
except Gino Pasterino
    an old man

Assures from
    that balcony
we looked
    down.

The noise the
    beach of parasols
obscures—
    the place

Gets no rest
    from the sea
it hides now
    —nor eyes.

Understanding:
    I wasn't going to say
for fear
    You didn't want to hear.

That's the worst
    of understanding,
a handshake
    would be better.

And of
    Antichi
there is
    no end.

That song
    is the kiss
it keeps
    is it

The
   unsaid worry
for what
     should last.

By the intimacy
    of eyes,
or its inverse—
      restiveness

Of heart—
    Pisa's Baptistry,
Nicollà Pisano's
    pulpit

Cannot—*antichi*—
    hold a candle
to light the
     circle of rock

Sculptures
    in the shadow
of round
    wall—

Primitive
    monumental
nameless
    as the carver

Who hewed—
    constraining
his shapes
    to rocks,

A lion and Judah
    perhaps,
a king—David
    by his harp,

The mother—
        married to
his line—
        her granite

Suckling
        the child—
manifest
        as the thigh

Of the
        Triumphant God
on the mosaic
        Judgment

Seat
        that Cimabue
directed
        in the semidome

Over the apse
        of the Cathedral
across
        the close.

Besides this
        seen that
legs
        would walk to

Duccio's
        chromatic story
in Siena's
        museum

Is subtle
        only
when lighting
        from

The green hills
        and knolls
the great and
        true candle

That lifts
        his countryside
which it lights
        today,

As, again, out
        of all
profluent
        Florence

A great cow
        of rock
on
        a plinth

In the Museo
        Opera del Duomo
is,
        first, valid,

More than any
        later takes
of Giotto
        in paint

And should be
        after the
stillborn
        recent ruin, a

Chapel
        in Santa Croce
selling gilt
        red leather bags.

Fra Angelico's brother
      painted one stiff
crucifixion
      after another

One
      in each
cell
      down one

Of two rows
      on the
top floor of
      San Marco

Each
      martyr's wall
his
      torture,

His
      angelic
brother
      who kneeled and rose

For the opposite row
      of cells
breathed the
      whole Legend:

A horse
      or a baby
two crossed trees
      or a mother,

In one fresco
      the luminous
center
      a piece of bread

The Lord of His
        own Last Supper
holds to the mouth
        of its inseparable Guest,

All who eat there
        inseparable.
For one afternoon
        looking down

From San Miniato
        on the flower
structure across
        the Arno

We may miss
        the Masaccio's
no distance below
        in the Carmine,

But
        if they are
for all time
        there will

Be another time,
        as in Rome
after
        the rising abstract

Of square
        futurist
coliseum,
        the Fall

Before
        the Decline
built a
        ruin to order

And Nobody's
    priority
of holes
    to come.

After
    Church
rose on
    the Forum

And this
    dug up,
churches
    fell

They square
    the marble
faced
    oval

And after
    Henry
qualmishly
    shy

Of Chaim
    (life)
and an Adams
    he read

Himself
    Adam
(earth)
    "–Why!

Why! !
    Why! ! !–"
Because
    his blood

Chilled,
    for whom
a Jew
    and friend

Is embarrassed—
    there is
other time
    repeating

Like his neighbor
    the blind beggar
on the steps
    of Ara Coeli

Altar of Heaven
    cypresses hide stars
candles shine towards
    cypresses

The column of
    Trajan so
small
    below

The grandeur is brutal
    only in the cast
in the Victoria
    & Albert.

Rome is a low
    city of shuttered houses
with
    tawny or orange views

Its older ruins
    so gentle
they disappear,
    to have been

Like the old brick
    Roman wall
that falls lower than
    any new apartment,

And the Pantheon's dome
    if stripped of its coffers
is but the adolescence
    of a geometry

That pours steel concrete.
    Familial, travelled,
or effeminate,
    the Romans loved

To possess and please
    not size so much as small
marbles of Greek gods,
    and also their wives

Daughters and sons: unlike
    the Christians
in the catacombs
    who burying theirs

In their walls
    must have turned
in distraction
    to give joy

To one another
    in carving
good shepherds
    and their flocks

Or painting fish
    or ravens
when their hymns
    and prayers

Brought no daily
        bread—and for fear no
other speech than
        out of their wild eyes.

Tendril vine
        stem
grape
        bud

Leaf flower
        the Roman work's
gentlest in
        the baths of Diocletian,

Stone skirts
        stone girl
drapes them on her
        wet and wind blown.

Farnesina
        stuccoes are
a snow's conceiving
        of white,

Four
        walls
of a room
        restoring Livia's

Villa Ad Gallinas
        carry continuous
garden, the green
        singing with birds

Where fruits shine orange.
        Stele
grow,
        mosaic

Tesserae
    animal and
abstract, each
    is animate.

In germ
    the ribbed vault
on a sarcophagus,
    also a tiny

Fan vault—
    so proportioned
as not to excite
    later doubts of lavishness.

So the unribbed
    vault at
San Vitale
    hints at the rib

But remains
    where
the eye can take in
    gold, green and blue:

The gold that shines
    in the dark
of Galla Placidia,
    the gold in the

Round vault rug of stone
    that shows its
pattern as well as the stars
    my love might want on her floor

The quiet better than crying
    peacock is immortal
she loves, knows
    it so pretty

That pretty in
    itself is enough
to love.
    She likes:

The Bell Tower
    in Venice
whose windows
    run not down

The center
    but along the side
edge; the three
    gonfalon

Poles before
    St. Mark's Basilica
like votive candles
    for the five

Kisses of the cusped
    lunettes
of the second
    story;

The bare south wall
    relieved by a tile
as tho it hung
    upon a wall at home.

Nothing is
    even,
so
    touches.

She
    came to Venice
by night
    a love that fears

Water
     and trusts the
stranger balance
     of the gondolier,

It is not a question
     with the red purple gold
of houses in water
     of a torture

Making paint stone
     or stone
wrongly
     flesh.

The Banda Municipale
     plays Boccherini's
"Menuetto"
     in the lit

Shadow of the night
     sky the roof of
the public reception hall
     of the Piazza

Ledges of
     whose palaces and church
crowd
     the pigeons asleep.

Bright to the morning
     they feed
on the swell
     of the Grand Canal

Who can drive past
     the new church of
Jesu Lavoratore,
     poor carpenter.

The faded
 fresco
in San Zeno
 of Verona,

Of the mourning
 of Jesus
down
 from the cross—

Eyes
 cannot tell
if leaves
 cover the weeping

Or if the mottles
 shred colors
where plaster flaked,
 never meant

For leaves,
 the statue
of San Zeno
 himself looks Buddhist,

And the Han-
 like carving
of the small sculptured
 squares of the bronze

Doors of San Zeno
 come much nearer
Heaven than
 Ghiberti's gates.

Of good company
 then
the screed
 is:

To Montecchio
    to eat well
for two houses
    'star-cross'd'

Or history is
    so
as the wrinkled
    signora in black

Head shawl
    says kindly
'the young from
    everywhere, as far as

America,
    come here for
Giulietta's Tomb'
    stand at

The broken lid
    (it might be
a bath)
    of the marble coffin,

A coil of
    climbing plant
comes down
    thru the grate

In the ground
    of the overhead cloister
to look
    also;

That Sunday is
    best to eat a
fruit and not
    cross the Adige

For the Roman theatre
    we see across it,
and not go
    to sit in the

Box
    of the Gens Valeria
where—a question if—
    Catullus sat?

Sirmio, almost the
    eye of islands
o Lydiae lacus
    Garda, gem,

Mine;
    this is it
which makes it
    worth it;

Three months go;
    that the innocent
pyramid of red and blue
    that suffers at the eating

Is for the movement
    of the hands to it
and the mind
    that willed to eyes;

One work of art
    to a room, the exhibit in
Milano's Sforzesco
    shows is enough;

The fresco
    or tempera
is, as of Luini,
    of green and wheat;

As on the other
        side of the Alps
the peasants
        meet Parliament;

Quiet;
        tilling;
the uplifted frozen
        wave of Pilatus;

A man
        tilling
mountain
        upland;

Liveable
        place;
whose character is
        endurable

As the eyes are moist before
        the regularly spaced
flower window boxes
        of Berne; the

Aare
        flows below, above the
old city
        old or new there's

No
        architecture
to speak of;
        walk.

Of travel's
        sickness
one's young son
        puns

Guiltless
      if world-
bred,
      'The reason

I threw up
      was not a Confucian egg
nor a Lao-tse but
      a bad egg.

How's *your* Duomo?'
      Returned to the sea
past point of no
      return

Leans over
      the deck rail—
'Not worth
      being sick for'—

It blows up
      its furtive hush
a sound that
      loses sound in

Blued white:
      'Lace.' Laundry.
'But'
      he says

'Can you
      describe it—
always
      different.'

Practice
      in lifeboat drill.
A baby in blue
      storm cape's

First to be wheeled
    off the gangplank,
the tug with something
    like a fig leaf approaches

The ship's bow.
    Go home.
There you may
    think of it.

The pyramid
    repeats
of the peaks.
    Colorado's *Red Rocks:*

The natural
    acoustics
of the amphitheatre
    between the two

Sandstone shapes
    they call
Creation
    and *Shipwreck.*

As the eyes
    near wreck
to create
    when they see

RAIL   CROS (S)
SING   ROAD
of pastime
    and good company.

I's (pronounced *eyes*)
[1937–1960]

(Ryokan's scroll)

dripping
words

off

a
long
while

the
first
snow

out
off
where
blue

      eyes

      the
      cherry
      tree's
      petals

Homage

Homage

Of love for, to
the young—

the old's affectionate
greetings—
young greetings
multiply

a few but so
significant greetings

occasioned attentions
all outs of

their green desire

loneliness
looking to
make friends—

when all the old
much too far away
to make friends
can do

is to befriend
each single
"good"
act

and
as part of
the world's
debt

place
it or a
nuisance too
much

in eternity
as it were
of
friendship

that could be
lovable
embodiment
if some after world

offered
as
in
time:

far
out of
the world

are the
old—

so much
the
new only
young

bodies
not
backed
by back aches

show
new
only.

Her Face the Book of—
Love Delights in—Praises

Pericles and *Two Gentlemen*

"will you give yourself airs
from that lute of Zukofsky?"

Praises Robert Duncan

"Yes, for I would have my share"

How will his praise sound back to him?
If I let it be
To confirm
One Henry Birnbaum
                and
                    quote
                        him.

        "I ought to thank
                Zukofsky,
        a wonderful voice,
                Zukofsky."

No, my young-old well-wisher,
The second in less than six months,
That makes not you,
"That makes me eclectic"
As tho arm in arm with me
May I say your songs run up to me,
Unstring insensible judges
In their mid-century
        With their Stock
Opera House of vocables—
None of us wants to sit in it—
Not I, 55, nor you, say, forward-looking
                        back to me,
To Father Huc's tree
Of Tartary
On which we are each leaves' Poetry

Where She a breath
Comes out of drudgery
Notes a worked out knee deck her daisies
And apropos of nothing
'There are words that rhyme but
are never used together
You would never use *lute* with *boot*'—
So she has used them.

Or again—
As where cheek touches forehead,
                    of face
        My father's *boot*
        by a *lute*
                with eight courses—
                I have rhymed
                        it:

To her face. Love delights, the book of praises.

Hill

        Black waters'
        November
        clouds
        high afternoon
        reflections
        fold, draw up
        wrinkle and
        web
        currents
        to white the
        plate steel
        cruiser
        run in
        black calm
        against
        a raised white
        swathe
        as tho for day
        the Milky Way
        fell
        around familiar
        island

        hill,
        autumn's mountain

1959 Valentine

The more that—
    who? the world
seeks me so
    to speak

the more
    will I
seek
    you.

Wire

Wire cage flues
    on
the roofs:

Paper ash—whole
    sheets
in gusts—

Flawed by winds
    fly
like doves

Motet

General Martinet | Gem Coughed A- | hem, and A- hem, and A-
hem De- | ploying the nerves of his | men Right, and about face,
to his phlegm.   Their | whangs marched up to the | sky, His
eyes telescoped in his head A | pillow that as | pillar of Eur-
ope He | flung to his rupture A- | head.

WORDS: L.Z.
MUSIC: C.Z.

Jaunt

1

Verona, Ohio
right 3 miles
highway is past
alfalfa

plain of corn
wheat, clover, rye,
slips of—

younglings of
peach, pear, apple,

weeping willows
hang down only
to bring up
maid Barbary's song

all at one side
all on a wall
orange
day lilies
pore as tho over
red—

evening

after their kind

alpha and omega

a first sight
of seven palomino
horses
white tails
out of their cream
bodies
almost sweeping
the ground

and as if
these are
human haunches
of an Eastern world

vines
bind the
landscape with who
named it Verona

after one
first trip to Europe
perhaps
reading
Two Gentlemen

Proteus and Valentine
or about the still
younger lovers
from fatal loins

male and female

imagining
one night

foreign farmer
or native teacher

2

The cow scraped by
the hood of the car
leaped its frightened
dung its avatar
that gentle
(not the hood)
the ungentle
driver
escaped.

3

49 states
filly
rearing on
the wind
3 ways

a little housewife
the lacy love

4

Rune

ruinin'
runs

Mexico

5

Physical
geography
a sea of cotton or
a fluff of icebergs or
waterfalls, trees, gigantic
mushroomed ivories
Chinese of whatever animal, or
huge herbs soar trunkless
banana trees

white

illusion it is slow
the aircraft humming
at 330 miles an hour
is 5 minutes passing

a plot of plan, delta, gulf
two glints of ships
over 20,000 feet below
or just as soon
there is no
earth, God's people
are below the clouds, His
sun above, the plane
banks over virtually
a field of Arctic snow
that with the rainbow to spare
skyscape promises better than landscape.

Peri Poietikes

What about measure, I learnt:
Look in your own ear and read.
Nor wrest knowledge
            in no end of books.
Pyrrhic nor *Pirke* do.
Mind, don't run to mind
boys' Greeks' metres gnome,
rummage in tee tomes, tee-tums,
            tum-tees.
Forget terms.
No count is sure,
more safe, more stressed,
more heard, or herds peace more
in world where hearing
is a going out
or instance up or down;
from in, different instance out.
Trust: to lip words
briefs what great (?) discourse well.

I's (pronounced *eyes*)

Hi, Kuh,

those
gold'n bees
are I's,

eyes,

skyscrapers.

*

Red azaleas
    make this
    synagogue
Not the
    other way
    round.

*

Fiddler Age Nine
(with brief-and violin-case)

Sir Attaché Détaché.

*

HARBOR

The winds
agitating
the
waters.

*

FOR

Four tubas
or
two-by-four's.

*

Angelo

the Superintendent's
Porto Rican Helper—

See
I work
alread' start roof pla'form
ñ scratching floor
on
Eight

if
I
can do
you
good.

*

SEVEN DAYS A WEEK

A
good man
when everybody
is draping
the flag on a holiday
he's behind a box

or stamp or information
window in the
Post Office.

*

TREE—SEE?

—I see
     by
          your tree

—What
      do you
           see

       *

    A SEA

     the
     foam
     claws

     cloys
     close

       *

    A B C

He has wit—
but who has more—

who looks
some way more

withal

than
one eye

weeps, his voice

       *

AZURE

Azure
as ever
adz aver

To Friends, for Good Health

(*Sneezing on it:*)

And the
best

To
you
too

After *I's*
[1961–1964]

Daruma

Daruma
found object
that is art

for good luck

         Peter's sen
         Ami
         Ren
Will:

a bit
of rock

air
fire
water
sun

slow
ember

when a
butterfly

became
his wings

aye

knew he'd have

to go
to you

seven (?)
years ago

wearing
the
jacket

I'm
wearing
here

Hear?

The Old Poet Moves to a New Apartment 14 Times

The old poet
moves
to a new apartment
14 times

1

"The old radical"
or surd—

2

I's (*pronounced eyes*)
the title of his last

followed by *After I's.*
"After"—*later* or
chasing?

222

3

All the questions are answered with their own words
intellect the way of a body a degree "before"
soughed into them

if the words say silence suffers less
they suffer silence
or the toy of a paradox

a worth less worth
than that *shall* will be said
as it is

4

Aleatorical indeterminate

to be lucky and free and original
we might well be afraid to think
we know beforehand exactly
what we're doing

rather let it happen

but the 'illogical' anticipation,

music, has always been explicit
as silence and sound have

in the question
how long is a rest to rest.

In the 'old' metered poetry
the Augustan proud of himself
jingle poet as he says it

freedom also happens
tho a tradition precounts

but someone before him
is counting for him
unless it happens

that the instant has him
completely absorbed in that someone:
a voice not a meter

but sometime a meter's a voice.

5

After all—
nothing
interests me
when it is full of being.

Ground,
what there's a little sun on.

Why any nuisance
to black it out?

6

Anger, an impetuousness of kicking
the four strings off the fingerboard,
blind led the bees.

7

Now a tray—
Achilles shield
great copper boiler end

from the furnace
in the home of her ma

stands burnished
at the door—
in the disguised center hole

(where the pipe support went thru)
made one with it

3 toy translucent
plastic horses
with Greek bangs

(Xanthus and Balius)

   but 3
Red behind Black
      and
favorite Yellow Sun between.

                8

      Tiny sarah golden
      so taken in

      by the beauties
      of the suites
      wondrously

      assumed
      her friends' new
      apartment

      had fabulously
      called in
      an interior decorator.

      She did not presume *they*
      knew nothing of decor

tho her loves
could they tell her so
had never aspired
to a decorator.

9

Back then
on Willow Street
"Happy," that is Pat

Pat
not for Patricia

(*Shall we not see
these daughters
and these sisters*)

Patrick, rickle
old man
collected garbage

singing
and no sooner
clean

than they dumped
it on him
again

in an incinerator
for which *they* paid
rent

it was his

whence this singing
ai ai ai ai

and carrying up
broken cartons
so they moved
with their books

as the brat
fourteen
the floor
below

wailed to her
banjo
and danced the twist.

10

A roof—
turned back on water
in sun holding objects
in sunny distance—

looked into sun
warmed the closed eyelids by it,
returned round to water
opened them on a blue
of water shadow of sky

when the street below
crowded with were they neighbors that *had*
lived there—as in a newspaper neared
human ashes icy roads
Auschwitz crematories'
scattering them from a cart
pulled by twenty children
and Angel Head Doctor whipping them
Head Death cycled along

was was whistling Mozart—

to La Paz, Bolivia
that Peace
where students shouted
in the court of a hospital to
a doctor on call—
treating victims,
"*Their* names,
give us *Their* names,"
were shouted at from inside:
"They're poor people
we cannot identify them
they do not have documents."

The roof—
mountain fallen molehill

had so much to do with so little
perhaps some syllables
'head lost
why cry "bald"'?

—that to move
helped necessity.

11

When the walls
are dismantled
realize
the horror
of dust

but also
where a curtain
kept the dust from
the walls,
a white

that with most
things packed shows how
little one needs
waiting for the movers

to come.

12

Who may not anymore
show his writing to friends
not till it's print
or his dreamed words
of trooped galaxies
a night of the day
they move in

glad some envy
stopped showing
its writing to him
art is not covetous
whose life is long

drip key and murky

so they compose
wet the ants

craft name
Friendship

rocket thrust
established in lbs.
300,000

weightlessness
about
4 hours
almost another
hour of minutes

only the top
half
of the pier
of the bridge

the top
half of
façade of
skyscraper

show from
the rise
of the lonely
street

float
　..

the water brings me all things
the valentine of
the sweet fat friend
so heavy he cannot carry his drawers

optimism gaining among steel men.

13

If the worst comes to the best
you'll have 'em all

is it better to carry a single fiddle case?
a case with two fiddles?
a consort is better?
it is perhaps lighter to carry a single one
for if not in its life
in that other of playing
the case shall be no bit of the fiddle
and the fiddle not with the case.

14

She brings me all things
the caryatid of the 10th floor
holding the 11th

goes up the stair
wearing out her little fingers
cleaning

and no one says
the pity of it

the water bringing all of the continents,
the oceans
otherwhere towards the windows

have we a terrace?
when the
sun comes in
it is the
Southeast

Atque in Perpetuum   A.W.

Alias to a wand the height lowered
sleep well who woke every half hour
on the hour with last breath joked
two legs were mine walk 'Glad to
hear your voice' 'Glad to hear my
own voice.' One shot and sat on
in the universe fast but unsure. Itself
sedum has come up thru rock water
slate black twilight the sky's blue reins
white sweats in mist rains storms summer
clears stars and moon rounds. We have
not walked out of this place what
have we to collect. Each privet's ablossom
I am a son of the soil.

A coast guard cutter with four orange
lights and a search- scurrying only a
boat's government and the world's raids. Wire
fence of high terrace meshes day and
night air altered sometimes by gulls swallows
helicopters and turbojets. It used to shower
Aprils but never blew winds that way.
The scholarly string player has a theory
of his tone the old hour listens
'I don't understand a thing you're saying
but it's terribly'—sleepily—'out of tune.'
Counting sevens an ornament unto my wound.

The

The
desire
of
towing

Pretty

Look down out how pretty
the street's trees' evening green
with the day's with them
on globular lights no Hesperides
was has fruit more lemony
orangey cherryie honeydew melon white
like several white sports cars
turned the corner no peachier
headlights blaze in dark sides
of a row of cars
half-parked on the sidewalk
while for once nowhere here
fruits smell sing the mechanics

The Ways

The wakes that boats make
and after they are out of sight
the ways they have made in water:
loops, straight paths,
to do with mirror-like,
tides, the clouds the deep day blue
of the unclouded parts of the sky,
currents, gray sevens or darker shadows
against lighter in and out weaving
of mercurial vanishing eights,
or imaginably sights
instantaneously a duration and sun,
and the leaping silver
as of rain-pelted nipples
of the water itself.

After Reading

After reading, a song

a light snow
a had been fallen

the brown most showed
knoll trunk knot treelings' U's

The Sound marsh water

ice clump
sparkling root etc

and so far out.

The Translation

Wonder
  once
whence
  mulier

woman—
  Latin
mens
  sounds

other
  sense
in
  native

homonym—
  my
love
  air—

mule-
  ier
hardly
  either—

who
  can
who
  can

know
  both
is
  short—

what
  does
Lewis and
Short

say—
   (from)
mollior—
   we

homonym
   mulley
or
   also

spelled
   mooley
why
   not

mool*ea*
   l, e, a
why
   l, e, y

spellers—
   of
Celtic
   origin—

U.S.
   a
polled
   animal

dialect
   English
a
   cow—

in
   U.S.
a
   child's

word
  moolea
or
  polled

(*adjective*)
  hornless
q.
  v.

(positive)
  mollis

Greek
  malakós
amalós
  mōlus

(confer)
  blaychrós—
(perhaps
  Latin)

mulier
  (*mollior*
comparative)
  mollis

movable
  pliant
flexible
  supple

soft
  delicate
gentle
  mild

pleasant—
    not
bad
    for

authority—
    in
shorts
    so

many
    authorities—
you
    know

what
    authority
is—
    when

short
    each
has
    authority—

Liddell
    and
Scott—
    we

little
    and
scotfree
    blaychrós

that
    is
weak
    feeble

(adverb)
  blaychrōs
slightly
  no

I
  don't
like
  that

my
  blood
can't
  endure

it—
  malakòs
leímown
  a

soft
  grassy
meadow
  amalós

light
  (slight
like
  seductive)—

but
  "a
cura
  della

moglie
  del
poeta,
  che

ha
   tratto
poesie"
   who

has
   picked
poetry
   from

mens—
   moglie
that
   would

be
   mulier
that
   would

be
   wife
that
   would

be
   soft—
a
   sleeping

breath
   sof-
t-
   t

Finally a Valentine

There is
a heart

has no
complaint

better a-
part

than
faint

so the
faintest

part of
it

has no
complaint—

a
part.

Catullus
(Gai Valeri Catulli Veronensis Liber), translated with Celia Zukofsky

[1958–1969]

Translators' Preface

This translation of Catullus follows the sound, rhythm, and syntax of his Latin—tries, as is said, to breathe the "literal" meaning with him.

The skip from 17 to 20 in the sequence of the poems is traditional, after the earliest codices, Codex Oxoniensis (late 14c.) and Codex Sangermanensis or Parisiensis (c. 1375). Modern scholars usually include carmen 18 (fragment 2 in our book) with the *fragmenta* of the canon, but omit carmina 19 and 20 as spurious.

C.Z.
L.Z.
Nov. 14, 1961

1

Whom do I give my neat little volume
slicked dry and made fashionable with pumice?
Cornelius, to you: remindful that you
used to dwell on my scantlings as something great,
in that time when one solitary Italian
you dared ransack all the ages in three—
Jupiter!—learned and laborious papers.
Care, as you did, somewhat for this little book,
whatever quality, patroness virgin,
may outlast a perennial cycle.

2

Sparrow, my girl's pleasure, delight of my girl,
a thing to delude her, her secret darling
whom she offers her fingernail to peck at,
teasing unremittingly your sharp bite,
when desire overcomes her, shining with love
my dear, I do not know what longing takes her,
I think, it is the crest of passion quieted
gives way to this small solace against sorrow,
could I but lose myself with you as she does,
breathe with a light heart, be rid of these cares!

2a

And for this I am grateful, as rumor had
it the quick girl was to the golden apple
that swiftly lowered her girdle long tied.

Lament, o graces of Venus, and Cupids,
and cry out loud, men beloved by Her graces.
Pass here, it's dead, meant so much to my girl, the
sparrow, the jewel that delighted my girl,
that lovable in her eyes she loved them less:
like honey so sweet he was sure to know her,
with her ever as a girl's with her mother;
not seizing a moment to stray from her lap,
silly crazy to hop up here and down there,
one endless solo to his only goddess.
Who now? it's hard to walk thru tenebrous flume
down there, where it is granted not one comes back.
On you be the curse of the blind and dead shade
Orcus, hell that destroys all beautiful things:
so you stole my beautiful sparrow from me.
Why pick evil? why my little fool sparrow?
It's your doing—my girl's own, darling's sweet
excellent eyes a little swollen and red.

Facile as can be the boat you see, my guests, says—
it was the fastest of a navy for its run,
nothing quite like it floating which had been a tree
that it could not outstrip, either its oars plying,
or—if the course sped—soaring, no slack of canvas.
To it the coast of menacing Adriatic
will not say no, nor islands of the Cyclades
and noble Rhodes, nor the horrible Thracian
Propontis, nor the truculent gulf of Pontus,
by which this that had yet to be a boat was then
a tree combed with leaves: for on Cytorus' summit
it swayed often to the sibilant talk of leaves.
Pontic Amastris and Cytorus where the box tree
grows, this you have witnessed and can witness yet,
my sailboat says; ultimately my origin
goes back to you, it says—it stood on your summit,
that those were your waters which first imbrued its oars,

and from there thru uncontrollable fretting seas
it sailed its lord, whether the winds hailed to larboard
or starboard, or as if to trumpet Jupiter
lit instantly astern to fill the favored sheets;
not a soul bespoke vows to the shore gods for her
when she came out in that furthest sea, nor all her
way here as she hastened to this unshadowed lake.
As said, this was *prior to:* and laid up in store
ages quietly and dedicates itself to you,
Gemini Castor and his twin-starred Castor.

5

May we live, my Lesbia, love while we may,
and as for the asseverating seniors
estimate them as one naught we won't assess.
Suns will hurry to set and will rise—likely:
but for us it all means when the brief light sets,
night is perpetual, and we are dormant.
Dear, kiss me a thousand times, then a hundred,
then another thousand, another hundred
and another thousand, another hundred,
and when we've roused that multitude of thousands,
confounding their number we will know no sum
of them that a malicious eye may envy
while it keeps counting the many times we've kissed.

6

Flavius—that delicate lass—to Catullus,
if she isn't simply illicit inelegance,
well, you'd talk, never pose a will to keep still.
But the truth is I don't know what feverish
slut scores such delights—so put out, to act fair.
No it wouldn't be you lying bereaved nights,
not quick to be quiet the couch is crying
Assyrian garlands, fragrance of olive
and pillows like pairs, in the thick of it, a
trite rubbing and trembling shaking the litter,

rustle of argument ambling up and down.
Now about this *that* that *is* you'll say nothing.
Why? it shouldn't take much to foot into the open
the slinking backside-before that you're hiding.
I don't care whether it's sinful or holy,
do tell us. For I want to take you and that
love of yours and invoke you both to the skies.

7

Queries, you ask how many times must I kiss
you, my Lesbia, what stint can requite us.
Numerous, the number of Libya's sands
on laserpitium-flowering Cyrene,
fiery Jove's oracle lies there opposite
veteran Battus in his sacred sepulchre,
or sidereal moult when the quiet night
looks over hidden embraces of lovers,
so much kissing, such multitudes of kisses
can and must satisfy insane Catullus,
numberless the curious may not count them
nor can evil tongues ever fasten on them.

8

Miss her, Catullus? don't be so inept to rail
at what you see perish when perished is the case.
Full, sure once, candid the sunny days glowed, solace,
when you went about it as your girl would have it,
you loved her as no one else shall ever be loved.
Billowed in tumultuous joys and affianced,
why you would but will it and your girl would have it.
Full, sure, very candid the sun's rays glowed solace.
Now she won't love you: you, too, don't be weak, tense, null,
squirming after she runs off to miss her for life.
Said as if you meant it: *obstinate, obdurate.*
Vale! puling girl. I'm Catullus, *obdurate,*
I don't require it and don't beg uninvited:
won't you be doleful when no one, no one! begs you,

scalded, every night. Why do you want to live now?
Now who will be with you? Who'll see that you're lovely?
Whom will you love now and who will say that you're his?
Whom will you kiss? Whose morsel of lips will you bite?
But you, Catullus, your destiny's *obdurate*.

9

Veranius of all my beloved friends
who stands, my eyes, before the truckload of them,
is anything in it this news that you're home
and one with your brothers and graying mother?
You've come home, O my message of beatitude!
I shall see you, hear you on the Iberians—
a narrative of lands, of facts, of nations,
as must be you—complying to the joyful
column of your neck, savor both mouth and eyes,
O how can it be I am the most blessed,
what is it makes me light with beatitude?

10

Varus old crony had me visit his love—
something else from relaxing in the Forum—
a little tart, so she seemed pent up as I was,
not so much without grace as not to show any.
We'd just come in and her talk came down on us
insurmountably varied, cute: what is it
like in Bithynia now, how are things managed—
anyway had I come home with some money.
I told her how things were, nil—why how could the
public along with praetors and their cohorts
all cap if off with an unctuous haircut,
when the top queer (of a) praetor there wouldn't
pillage a hair of his rump for a cohort.
"In any case," it continues, "couldn't be
that in their native scene you did not fare with
a couple of litter bearers." I go out to the girl
with a face one might call beatific,

"No," I chime, "I was not so unfortunate,
vile as that province was luck set me down in
I had a posse of eight erect bearers."
Not that I ever had a bearer there or here
able to load down his neck with the fractured
veteran leg of a low grubby settee.
As you'd expect the girl's kindling: an idea
or I'm wrong: "my sweet Catullus, please, a little
one of those for me would be just commodious,
I'm off for Serapis, man, now." "Phew! Well," I say,
"is that what I said? it's a bit mixed up as
to my having—I spoke too fast: my side-kick,
Gaius, Cinna to you—it's his appanage.
Really whether his or mine, what's that to me—
with authority to use them as my own—
you're too insultingly silly to be lively
when you hint that my little lie craves negligence."

11

Furius, Aurelius: comities—Catullus.
If he penetrate most remote India,
lit as with the long resonant coast East's wave
          thundering under—
if in Hyrcania, mull of Arabia,
say the Sacae, arrow ferocious Parthians,
why even the seven gamming mouth, colored
          ichor of Nilus—
even that Transalpine graded tour magni-
fying visions of our Caesar's monuments,
Gallic Rhine, and the horrible ultimate
          mask of the Britons—
on hand, men, come whatever gods ferret and
want of us, you who're always prompt to feel with
me, take a little note now to my darling,
          no kind word dictates.
May she live, and avail herself, in the moist
clasp of one concourse of three hundred lechers,
loving no man's ever, and doomed to drain all
          men who must rupture:

no, let her not look back at me as she used to,
at her love whose fault was to die as at some
meadow's rim, the blossom under the passing
    cut of the share's thrust.

12

Marrucinus Asinius, that sinister
hand of yours is no belle with a joke or wine—
nor that linen toll lifted from negligents:
How spiced is your wit? Just fidgety—stupid?
qualmish, sordid and entirely wanting in taste.
Won't you credit me? Then credit Pollio
your brother whose pure heart would contribute a
talent to undo your theft: nice well-mannered
discerning boy who's correctly facetious.
Choir of three hundred hendecasyllabics—
expect it, if you won't let go my handkerchiefs;
what moves me about them is no estimate:
Mnemosyne is the true judge of friendship.
These Saetaban handkerchiefs from Iberia
were sent here to remind me of Fabullus
and Veranius: like my love's necessities,
thoughts of Veranius and my Fabullus.

13

Canapés, my Fabullus, at home any
day now, if the gods don't want you to diet—
say that you come here bountifully laden
with canapés, not without cither girl, with
wine and salted wit, cacophonous laughter,
if you come to us so, magnanimously ours,
you'll eat canapés: need Catullus tell you
his little sack of plenty's Arachne's web.
In return accept love's order of merit,
what is more suave or invested with elegance:
as for unguent, my boy, there will be my girl's—
her donors the Venuses and the Cupids—

251

when you smell a whole whiff of it you'll beg the
gods to fancy you, all, Fabullus, all nose.

14

Not that I look to my eyes more than your love,
your kindness is to me, Calvus, immune to
your gift that's as odious as Vatinius:
how, why have I gone wrong, quipped what so luggish
to incur perdition from these deadly poets?
May he stall in his malice, your mule client,
who toted you to their misfit emporium.
I'm inclined to suspect this new award or
bonus is a sub rosa fee from that lit-
erator Sulla; not half bad, I'm lucky
you're paid, your labors have not been disparaged.
Gods, what a horrible unholy little volume
you, think! I must say *you* sent to Catullus—
not miscounting that the day he should perish
would be the First Saturnalia of all days!
No, no joke, titbit of wit can save you a bit:
when luxurious dawn comes to the bookstalls
I'll run, screen them off—Caesii, Aquini,
Suffenus, the whole venomous lot of them,
and with these subtleties remunerate you.
Void, vile, now be interred, and goodbye to you
ill look into hell where your dead feet led you,
incommodious cycle, pests of poets.

14a

Say quite by chance there's one sees these ineptitudes
my readers to be and with such hands as might
touch never horrified to move toward us

15

Commend to you my cares for the love I love,
Aurelius, when I'm put to it I'm modest—
yet if ever desire animated you, quickened
to keep the innocent unstained, uninjured,
cherish my boy for me in his purity;
I do not hint that "people"—nothing we fear
from those, flitting in the street's mad crook or look,
racing appearances of seeming occupied:
the root of my dread is that your prurience
corrupts, festers in good and bad youth alike.
Whale as much as you love it, love it, and move it—
incontinence out always for the public pry,
only please spare this one boy your impudence.
But let mind's malice cote your furious course—
intentions so impelled, salacious, culpable,
as are insidious to us, what lashes
will come down on your head—your malicious fate:
a traction on chained feet, the town's portcullis,
harried then, raped by radishes and mullets.

16

Piping, beaus, I'll go *whoosh* and I'll rumble you
pathic Aurelius and catamount Furius,
who mix my versicles with your poor tasties—
the sound is a mollycoddle's, I'm not up
to par for chasteness. But the pious poet
is chaste, his versicles not nailed to his need,
quick to themselves with no lack of decorum,
if the sound models not quite pure for pudency
what incitement it carries passes into
now I won't say hairless boys', but such hoary
necks as endure not quite up to feel lumbar.
Milling thousands of kisses are base or make
me out some mare of a male—you impute that?
Piping, beaus, I'll go *whoosh* and I'll rumble you.

17

O Colonia, whose wishes build a long bridge to dance on,
for all dreamed sallies and parries, your fear is how inept are
the crude pinned legs of your little bridge, a raised stance without axis,
that supine they'll sink in the bog, be polluted recumbent;
make it good your long new bridge that spans libidinal fiat,
go well with Salisubsilus, sacred rites, skipping canter:
mind you, see then I have my laugh, Colonia, that rises
when the damn municipal mute on your bridge—whom I want to
steer off, lunge tumbling into mud, head first the cue to feet last—
percolates, all of him, your lake's most total paludal puke,
its most livid and maximum muck of its profoundest bog.
He has no salt in him this man, not the least sap, the instarred
tremulousness of a two-year old rocked in his father's arm.
Could come if he is there to his vernal flower of a wife—
girl more delicate than the docile hide of a kid, she's a sure
wonder not to be neglected more than the blackest of grapes—
lets her hanker where she wants, he's not one hair displaced by facts,
not the least elevated on his part, hewn the felled alder
in the foss *here lies* lamed in the hip by Ligurian axe,
tantamount to a sense of all as if she were not at all,
it's the tale of this mess, stupor sees nothing, he hears nothing,
if he is it, whether it and not it, no question knows it.
Now him I'd like to catapult from your bridge, measure him prone
to see if it's possible to excite his stolidity,
that supine mind of his, sunken derelict of grave channel
mud tenaciously sucking him in like a mule's iron shoe.

21

Aurelius, father, assure that the o numb
gnawn hungers' odious quota of errant
ort, sump, alias the years' runt of anise,
pea to caries scoops my love to such mores.
No clam when you smile the joker is you now,
adheres to him, his life owns your experience.
Frustrate: not so insidious an instrument—
the tang of it to me's your prior rumbling.
If your stomach were sated I'd be tacit:

its announcements keep me doleful, could assure
me my poor boy will sit there, learn how to thirst.
Quarry designs to a licit pudency,
or you will rumble face down for a finish.

22

Suffenus is, stay Varus,—whom you've proven—is the
o most Venusthewed, active ax what, urbane as—
his damn cue's long reams of preoccupied verses.
Put his goal at ten thousand, some decked out plural.
Poor script, eh? not so it fit incest in palimpsest—
realloted: quires, regal eye, new cylinders,
new little umbiliform roll ends, rubric lore, thongs,
membranes ruled plumb o (my) all equated with pumice.
How come legible as it is and urbane as
Suffenus he's one Capricorn milked cuss, fusser,
rear sass of hate or ton of bore the hack mutates.
How could he put it that messy? modish scurry
seeks out the dog with the raciest word batter,
yet then the fag's there tossed in, face it, the rural
facsimile tugs at a poem; no quiet aim—
a quest, to be at his poem, calmed if scribbled:
to make it good then he's all self-admiration.
Not wonderful, we're fallible; no quest quizzed that's
not allocated reveries of Suffenus—
possess so quickly our attributes of error:
nor do we see the knapsack on our back's the ghost.

23

Furius, with no key to service, no key
to strongbox, bedbug, spider, hiss of fireplace,
who rooms with father, stepmother, their quorum
of teeth which can well make comestibles of
flint, you're lucky, you, living with your parent
and come-conjugal-ligneous his partner.
Marvellous how hale each one of you can be,
your tried stomachs don't conk out, you'll yield no mite

to incendiary, nor to grave ruins,
furtive impieties, dolorous venom,
all like cases of fears allied with perils.
Ah your corporal humor's drier than horn,
outsits what major arid dooms habit is—
solar, frigid; assured, to eat is nothing.
Where then may you not be accounted blessed?
For you sweat's abeyance, saliva absent,
mucous suppressed with pituitous noses.
Add to this cleanliness the cleaner mundane
anus, cool purest little saltcellar lost,
net proceeds a case hardly ten times a year,
harder than a bean or fob of lapillus;
that, how much you may rub it, cannot fritter
and come off on a finger hinting possession.
Hike to commodious time, blest Furius,
no lees spurn the air in the pot for poor wine—
sesterces? to solicit precariously?
cant them! designs? Enough said is blessed.

24

O quick floss silk of the Juventii, form,
known heir, mode of such caught as if they weren't,
out posthaste and who ail to run on in ease:
my luck! had you instead divided Midas's
wealth with *this* who decks no service, nicks arc of
coin—whom sick to sink for you slobber in mire.
"Kid, isn't he a beautiful man?" you ask. He's:
said belle who decks no service, nicks arc of coin.
Yoke to him, love it, agh bicker or leave it:
he has no servant, he'll bite, nick arc of coin.

25

Conniving Thallus, mulley, you, cony cully, cop below—
well, anserous medulla, well immolated auricula—
well, pain and languid older sense, see, too extraneous—o so—
and then qua Thallus, turbid air, rape packing off, a hell of

come diva mull over Aries—oscine oscitancy,
remit my pallium to me, it's mine, vile blast who stole it—
my Saetaban sudarium, my Thynian tinct catagraphs—
inept—why palm them off as their sole heir whom time awaited:
wined unctuous sopping pup, give them to us, glued tines remit them,
now let your lathy cully bottom, menacing coddled hands
so used to turpitude be flagellated in this scribbling,
and insolently toss a minute at my will magnified
and soon dispensed with in a marring sea and in insane wind.

26

Furius, "Little Villa" has no nod for Auster,
flaw to oppose a taste naked to Favonius,
nor sighs with Boreas, out Apheliotes,
worms eat and mill it fifteen thousand two hundred.
O vent them horrible, I'm out quite, pestilent mm.

27

Minister wet to lee, pour the Falernian
and gear me chalices, ah by bitterest,
the law's Postumia, you bet magistral,
eh breezy kin a grape-loving breeziness.
Adieus qualifying between water and
wine are pernicious, let the odd serious
migrate: high! pure the thing on us 's the wine god's.

28

Piso's own comates, his, corps an inane as
opt sad sarks—kin no less—'at's expedited!
Veranius hoped, my—he took my Fabullus,
what rare rheum's to greet us? Sneezing come as tho
that vapid prig's cue to famine's to last you?
Equity's damned now to bills, potted, look, hell: the
expenses! with me qua my own, so cute is
my praetor, refer o datum, look well o,

"O Memmius, between me—you did this spine numb,
total travesty—leaned us—ire's ram, nasty:"
said quantum with eh-oh! pairs a few as 't is
casual, names nil by no minor warp of
arty "ease-up" as 't is. Pet noble amigos!
That woe pay this malice, dear gods and goddesses,
dent those reprobates, Romulus and Remus!

29

Whose hoax to put up with, outstare, protest patience,
no—see impudicity, voracity, a low,
Mamurra may bare what Comata Gallia
habited and top off with ultimate Britain?
Kin, hide of Romulus, how could you *see*, "It fares,"
yes impudicity, voracity, a low?
What, will an hunks' superb cheat's superfluity
perambulate a bit in all cubicles, a
white dove loose in the columbary—Adonis?
Kin, hide of Romulus, how could you *see*, "It fares"?
Yes—impudicity, voracity, a low.
In whose name, imperator, did you, unique as
few stay, stake your goal, the most distant west island,
so that your vested futtock of a Mentula
make comestible two to three thousand liens?
Is it allied sinister liberality?
Power homes on patronage for a poor haul is it?
Paternal principal first, lanced to the bone, but good:
secondly prey out of Pontus: in the third haul
Iberia, one skit—auriferous Tagus.
And causes Gallia to tremble and Britain,
why do you love this hunks? Could he, put to the test,
not sink then or not devour our patrimonies?
In whose name, in Rome's or that of base opulence—
so cur genders cur, do you foredoom Rome and all?

30

Alfenus, remember *kind intimacies?* false? They elated us,
I am not to commiserate, rue a dull kiss—and to be cool?
I'm—my prodigal, I am not to doubt failure or perfidy?
Men's false acts, human impieties, leave the Gods cool in the sky?
Why do you neglect them, desert me to misery and malice;
ah, you! what end to men face, whom have they then, what faith
                                                    to feed them?
Care to do as you bid, animus trod there by iniquity,
inducing me to love more and more as tho all love were *for* me.
And now you take them all back, yourself and your words and
                                                    their acts as
winds that irritate, carry a thick nebulous air—you've seen it.
Say you have blotted us out, yet the Gods remember, and Faith does—
why, they post to you this moment making you repent that fact too.

31

Peninsular arm, Sirmio, insular arm, well-
ing eye, kiss come to what in liquid won't stagnate,
mark of the vast fare and tugging that Neptune is,
how I'm to live into your light I've come to see;
it strikes past credence: Thynia and Bithynian
plains lie back of us, and I am safe here with you.
O what most solves us but that the blessed cure is—
comes when the mind's onus, repugnance, peregrin
labors, festerings vanish, no lair or nostrum—
desire we must acquiesce to, of our own bed?
O that's what in sum makes our labors most tempting.
Salve! o Venus-tied Sirmio, I choir your good,
good that the waters choir—Lydia's lake won't die:
redoubt, laugh! what what's homey crackling every room.

32

I'm a bow, my dual kiss, Ipsithilla,
my daily key, eye, my eye's little leap-horse,
you bid me to "when," I'm your meridian.
That: so you see as sure as that adjuvant,
no case, limb, menace obscure your tableland,
no tidbit love you outdoors far as a bier.
Stay home, my man he asks we pair us—no bis—
nine continuous gasps, no refutations.
Very, so he could, yes start if you bid to:
he's primed now a joke-stuffed satyr, so pin us!
pert under the tunic, pulling up the quilt.

33

Offer 'em up to me—bullneck crook of the baths
Vibennius Pa and Son, hide of filly—
Pa's dexterity not more or less inquiline
than Son's cully filly butts are voracious:
curs'd exile on them, some molluscan morass!
it is when all's said and done, Pa's trick rapine's
a nuisance to people, and the napped piles of
the filly no asset worth any vendor.

34

Diana, sum us in faith a-
like pure girls and boys we greet you,
Diana, pure boys and girls, we
    sing to you as you count us.
O Latonia, most to my
great lord Jove his own child, o his,
for whom your proper mother lay
    beside Delian olive,
meant you reign mistress of mountains
silverarmed forests whirring green
gullies escaping eyes, and their runs
    making the constant hum.

To Lucina condoling as
Juno pangs of bearing mothers!
to potent Trivia at night's
        dictate, o lumined Luna!
To your course, goddess, man's true year
mating each month's round to woman!
stack high and cool the reaping man's
        intact full fruits of harvest.
See we count on you! placated
sanction your own name; Romulus go
on, old quiet, so light's no bone
        such as might spite the gentle.

35

Poet I'm too near your and my sod daily—
well I'm, Caecilius, as this papyrus asks—
when *may* you come to Verona, relinquish
Como's new limits and the Larian lake?
Now with some value in my cogitations
we may keeping at them save you and myself.
Wary, so sapient, the way'll worry a bit,
grown wise to the thousand wiles of a girl
shunting, revoking the man she has collared,
ambushed in both hands that beg *more, more's rarer;*
why if the news is true which tunes me to her,
all *for* him, she dies for one passionate *more:*
intemperance caught by her first look at his
Lady Dindyma, she won't miss then—little
interior fires ignite, eat her medulla.
I know how it is, little Sapphic girl, the
Muses' Doctor: it's a hymn of a newest
Caecilius first starting his *Magna Mater.*

36

Annals of Volusius, cock at his offal,
won't you solve it this promise of my darling—
now sanctified Venus and her son Cupid
have her vow: if it so be her lover comes
back again, quits darting his squibs of iambs,
the most elect mess of the pest of poets,
she'd deed *his* scripts to tardy-limping Vulcan
to be burnt like all fruitless outlandish wood.
That's like my little testy darling's wit, its
jokes that leave the worst to the divinities.
Come o cerulean creation, ocean's
Venus sung to in Idalium, Urii's squalls,
Ancona, Cnidus round in reedy noises,
as holy in Amathus as in Golgi,
queen of Dyrrhachium, Hadria's tavern,
account the vow was doomed to be redeemed—wit
is no ill pendant off the neck of Venus—
let's without fuss at once set fire to this sham
plenty of forced jokes, rude country faggots, these
Annals of Volusius, cock at his offal.

37

Salt hacks, tavern boys, what skews, can't you burn alleys
on to your ninth pole from the Pile Hats Brothers Pillar!
So you'll put it as men you're first and last whoppers,
souls liquoring, cuddling what's puled in little arms,
conn future bawdry, put it 'other caterers irk us'?
Incontinent air, wood, seated asses, sulk a
century, two centuries, and what assurance
I can't run thru two hundred rumps, my assessors?
I'd quip at that: name tagged to his whopper on the
front of the tavern, scorpion wee boys, *inscribed!*
My little one, ah me, she sins to forget me,
and that much love a quantum of bitter nothing,
procuress after magnificent belligerence,
conceded—this thick. Hangs bony but is thick with

all men—a mite loves, acquits her indignities—
all pusillanimous moochers of cemeteries:
to that prat of all men the one pileated
coney, cool lousy Celtiberian filly,
Egnatius, opaque whim of bone and faked beard, and
bared dentures rinsed with a wash of Spanish urine.

38

My last—Cornificius—your Catullus'—
my—his last breath—by Hercules how laborious,
making, making it any day now some hour.
Come to! what minimum facile minim's quest.
consolation as a late allocution?
Ear I score—to be sick—my, so amorous?
Poor what lame love it be, allocution as
misty as, lachrymose as Simonides.

39

Egnatius, candid as his horse-bit white dentures,
grins right on, cocksure cockeye. Say a rare venting
sobselling counsel's oratory squeeze folk tears,
he'll grin right on. Sad pious raging feeling,
look at her! all but laid out with her son—mother!
he'll grin right on. Quick wit test, you become quest,
code come quack it, he grins it. Hunk, a bit more bum,
nor quite elegant (or I'll bite) nor urbane ham,
beware, my own doom tests me, bonny Egnatius!
Say you were urban ass or Sabine or Tiburtine
or pork of Umbria or obese Etruscan
or Lanuvian as dark as the teeth are white
or Transpadane, I mention my folks and tingle,
or what you love that laves his teeth in pure water,
the man who grins always cocksure I'd nullify:
no rise is so inept as laughter that oughtn't last.
Now, kid, you're Spanish: Celtiberia's the country
where to ease micturition, solace of morning

dint by itself brushes teeth white and frays red gums,
so the more highly polished extra large teeth are
by that more ample was the predictable lotion.

40

What demented malice, my silly Ravidus,
eggs your pricked conceit into my iambics?
What god not too benign that you invoked would
care dream your parrot's skit of ire and ruckus?
And it wants to purr in the public vulva?
What wish to live it up, be noticed—apt as
air is, squandering in my love's amorous
vice longer than you wished it, marred but poignant.

41

Ameana pulling, a foot touted high,
touched me for all of ten thousand: and popped scut
is the tour-pickled, low-puling long nosed, ah
decocted heiress of the milked Formiani.
Propinquity, quick buss this fuel, cure eye,
amigos, medicos, call convocations:
no nest, *she* is nuts, pulls her neck, rogue harried,
what lies sit solid ice imagine o some.

42

At hest, hendecasyllabics, what is this
ominous indignity, Quotas, is this ominous!
Joke? on me! but assay her madcap purpose—
nagged me (vestal!) is ready to tear you, my
pugilist arias! Pat? See you test this.
Pursuing her game don't flag or she'll tame us.
"Who's *she*, where is she?" A low qualm who'd date us,
turpitude in her rear, mimicking molested
ridden cat with a leer of a Gallic canine.
Come, your insistent claim, don't flag at Ate!

"Mad cat put it there, ready could you kill us!
ready, put it there mad cat, could you kill us!"
Known ass is factious? O looting, lupine whore,
out! See the dirtiest pot is its essence.
Say, there isn't a name chokes this pudendum.
Would see (no?) a lady's rubescence rim her
fierce canine mouth, maim us as much as a ray?
Come, clamorous tittering unaltered voices,
"Mad cat put it there, ready could you kill us!
ready, put it there mad cat, could you kill us!"
Said now my fickle profit, 'no guile'll move her.'
Mute and dusty rot, o muddy as could be,
see! quit! progress shows how ample your test is:
"Pwtty cat, prob-i-ty, ready you kill us."

43

Salvé, next, minimal, poor little nosey,
next below, padded foot, no grace of black eyes,
next longish digitals, next aura, sick o
not synonymous with an elegant tongue,
decocted mistress of a weak Formiani.
In the Province they think—now rate—you a belle?
Take you for Lesbia, compare you to her?
O cycles of fashions, yet the facts hate them!

44

O farm, dear nest, or say Sabine, ah say Tibur's,
(now addressed Tiburtine it means the wish, *no nest
accord Catullus more, love there;* quibbles core dust,
so pig who pins Sabine on him—ass, contendent)
say it, say Sabine, sieve verity it's Tibur's:—
full bent there in coming to in your suburban
villa, my lungs expectorate, expel a tussis,
not unmerited, come by my high me, my venter,
doomed sumptuous appetite, dead it'd cane us.
Now Sestius and this doomed wish to eat—convivial
I read him, *on Antius petty tyrant,* rum

plain numb and venomous pestilential logic—
hit me, the grave! a frigid frequence of tussis,
quashed, shaking and done in, a bosom fugitive
I sought my cure there of your urticaceous calm.
Whereat refected, my unscathed thanks as gratis
I go, my farm that did exculpate the pig I
am: yet pray, cronies, if the nefarious script of
Sestius tries me again, then grave and cough toss him—
not me, *said* (you see) *Sestius*—ferret the freak
whose tongue wagged me to eat his glum liver logic.

45

Acme, Septimius, sighs so amorous,
tenoned, sighing agree, "my" and quiet "Acme
knee too pretty to mar, what qualm, I pore oh
on my sum I see due, and if years part us
a wan tomb cool my pluck, may it perish
solus in Libya or India, tossed a
case of—went and met with a blue-eyed lion."
Woke who ticks it, Amor, sinister, right anti-
dexter, stern to wit, sneezed *him* approbation.
What? Acme laughed—the air-capped head, reflections
and all kiss—pure air, brow, kissed his welling eyes,
her love pure, pure red mouth saving what they had
"sic" and quiet, "my wit's heart, Septimille,
how can we do more than ask we serve Him who's
a tumult in me, my or a cry who quick-
ens—the God my love—sweetheart when he meddles."
Woke who ticks it, Amor, sinister wit anti,
dexter, stern of wit, sneezed *her* approbation.
Now off auspiciously the bond no praefect
to moot who animates a mount, a mounter.
And name Septimius, 'my soul is Acme
my wealth counts Syria's and Britain's squalid':
you know in Septimius faith deals his Acme
fact that delights as living hint and its queues.
Who's he allows anyone better pleasures,
vies with this Venus her auspicious theorem?

46

Warm gale, a dose of spring—revert to the pores,
hum, calm the roar of equinoctial skies,
you can do this, Zephyrs, who solicit hours.
Link—wander in Phrygia, Catullus—come by
Nicea's acres ripe over its hot sigh:
ah the clear sights of Asia claim us—our pace!
How my mind pries, traipses, avid vagaries,
how my light feet study, the pathway goes scant.
O good luck, comates, my of late decoyed, so
long a ways the same lane from home—those prospects,
diverse ways we eye rush back to report on.

47

Porky and Socration, two-eye sins as try
Piso's hand, scabies' famishing mandate,
why's Veranius low, Fabullus lower
warp t'this prepossessed lopsided Priapus?
Whose convivial loud and sumptuous long
day do you faggot as my old salt dollies
inquire around, three ways for invitations?

48

Mellowed *those*, I call *those* eyes, Juventius,
see, kisses may see into whose cue, pass, bar
whose cue, millesimal passions trek on, the
next mooned qualm, we, they are sight or what futures,
known, see dense, see, or arid as harvest is
kissed dry as we guess what a cool lot corn is.

49

Master of eloquence and Rome's potent line,
quote soon quote who fared quickly, Marcus Tully,
quote who'll post always a run into annals,
greatest yet to be makes my thanks—Catullus
accedes—the mere pusillanimous poet,
taunted—the mere pusillanimous poet
counts you too as his optimum of patrons.

50

Yesterday, Licinius, what a day it was
melting, losing us—might say—in my tablets,
we'd convene at our ease yet so delicate:
scribes and their versicles took their turns strumming,
lauding both that their numbers might hawk, might look,
redden as mutual, paired jokes with quaff of wine.
Ah what a link abides too, o I'll pore on—
incensed, Licinius—faggots these squibs of
wit, next my misery to keep us nourished,
no sleep tug quiet at the well of eyes, the
bed's total indomitable furor leagued to
worse errors, cooped in weigh there till light look in,
you could take them from me: talk smiling the same.
And I fester, labor who remember posthu-
mously, more to allay this jockied bed, to
joke again, friend: to be this poem's fay key,
ask your perception mime my dolorous hymn.
No audacious cavil, precious quaint nostrils,
or we must cavil, dispute, o my soul's eye,
no point—as such—Nemesis rebuffs too, is
the vehement deity: laud her, hang cavil.

51

He'll hie me, par *is* he? the God divide her,
he'll hie, see fastest, superior deity,
quiz—sitting adverse identity—mate, in-
    spect it and audit—
you'll care ridden then, misery hold omens,
air rip the senses from me; now you smile to
me—Lesbia's aspect—no life is to spare me
    [voice hoarse in a throat]
linked tongue set torpid, tenuous support a-
flame a day mown down, sound tone sopped up in its
tinkling, in ears hearing, twin eyes tug under
    luminous—a night.

51a

O the time, Catullus, to be molests you:
o tedious exults in you, in your quaint jests.
O the time it rages pre-us, to be at us,
    peers who died, or orbs.

52

Quick death, Catullus! what more horrors may hurry!
Salient in curule struma Nonius' seated,
pure consul undone by the rot of Vatinius:
quick death, Catullus! what more horrors may hurry!

53

Risible nice go when from mud a crony
quickly confirms the case against Vatinius
discriminating Calvus made explicit—
all admiration hikes its hands in tolling,
"Loving Gods, that tiny man's dissertation!"

54

Otho's scooped nut its pusillanimity,
Erius' rustic semen-looted cruor,
subtile, levitating petite fume who's Libo,
see, no? if this phenomena incurred your
bite and Fuficius' senile recoction.

54a

Irascibly iterating my iambics—
unmerited, unique eh—imperator.

55

A rum asks—see, fortune won't molest you—
day, man, strays—may you be seen to that thin bra?
We quizzed the Campus a wistful minor,
the Circus, then the omnibus book labels,
and even the Temple summit—Jove's sacred;
in our Magnate's milling ambulatory
fame mellows the girls—I'm keyed and preen, friend—
quasi vulture with eye to mind serene.
Ah, well, to sick you—see, flagged at a bum,
"Camerius my own—pass him my—pugh, you lie!"
One unquiet nude whim reduced and peaked us,
"Unh, hick, in roses' light at pap he lies."
So that I'm fair Hercules' labors' hest.
No custom brass like the fin guard Cretan,
no seen Pegasus o fair roar full at you,
no Ladas ego, pinnatepacing Perseus,
no Rhesus' team, snow-white kith, equine, big eye,
ad hoc plumipeds, those volatile askew,
winds, a rum crew, so mill require you course 'em—
whoso winked us, Camerius, would deed me your cares,
do face us, tame in all my bones, I'm dull as
with some mulish languorous paresis,
I swim to make your quarry to rive under.
Ten times ten faster you deny me a key?

Tick! no beast who bids his future rues, heyday
ah doctor! commit your credo, look it!
Name the lacteal girls whose tenant you lie?
See, lingua clouts a tenseness and orates,
fruits projects of Amor, a rise to all men:
verbose a goad of Venus. Low—quail! ah
well, see, wish, lick at obscurant palate, dumb
just thrive, see this party keeps amorous.

56

O ram ridicule home, Cato, the jokes some
dig, now cool your ears so the two cock in—no.
Read: they quick, kid, almost as Cato, Catullus:
raciest ridicule it may not miss jokes.
Prehended a mode of pupa, loon boy lay
crux on to her: and cog I, so placate Dione,
pro tale, o rig it all, me I cogged kiddie.

57

"Pull! crew"'s convenient to reprobate kin hides,
Mamurra pathic queer as Caesar a queer.
Neck mere whom: maculae pair as you'd risk queer
urban altered to a lad of Formiae and
impress a resident nick, well, you enter:
more pus at parity, game male who'd trick you,
you know in delict cool o erudite little ambush,
no qualm in lad or mug as whore is adulterer,
rivals, associates, pulling little girls' arms.
"Pull! crew"'s convenient to reprobate kin hides.

58

Caelius, Lesbia new star, Lesbia a light,
all light, Lesbia, whom Catullus (o name
loss) whom his eyes caught so as avid of none,
none else—slunk in the driveways, the dingy parts
glut magnanimous Remus, his knee-high pots.

59

Bononian, sis Rufa, Rufus' lum fell at—
this whore of Meneni siphoning sepulchers,
you've witnessed her rape scraps from dregs of caked kindlings,
come vaulting down ignited, roast quean for her pains
slapped by the unshaved corpse-burner who knows a story.

60

None but a lioness moaned this, Libya's mountains,
what Scylla's lot, trance, infamy of anguish, parted,
demented, dure, ah procreated like hatred,
you'd stop his pleas invoked in new wishes, curse so
contempt buries, and not miss, fiery cored heart?

61

Who lives o on Helicon hill,
coulter, as Urania's son,
quick reaps his shy bride for her groom,
virginal, o Hymenaee Hymen,
        o Hymen Hymenaee,

cincture your temples with flowers
suave o lent taste of marjoram
flaming caper light us, hook,
hook and veil, snowy foot wears, in
        light up the yellow sock—Whom

excite to hilarity, day
nuptial all day, a conch in song
woke, a harmony, tinkling, light
pelting humus, foot beat, mind your
      pine cone, hand, quaking tidings.

Now come Vinia, Manlius
call his Idalium—holy she
went to the Phyrgian, Venus
judged by him—boon become boon, and
      you wed, alit your virgin,

floret is well lit and attains,
myrtle is Asia ramulose,
whose Hamadryades dye, eye,
lead their games, sieve with rusk a dew,
      nutrient hue more ray.

Quire, go hook adit and fare hence
purge your link of the Thespiae
rubasse, Aonia's species,
nymph a cave's super ear a gat
      freezing runs' Aganippe,

and come home domain that woke her,
can you guess, keep the man, know how,
mean the more to him and keen as
ivy wax on the tree, hooked, hook,
      arbor implicate errands!

Sway in time the while, intact
virgins, keep you sweet, soon! when it
is your day! sing in the mode in-
diting it "o Hymenaee Hymen,
      o Hymen Hymenaee."

That love wend, his own audience,
seek to hurry here, out to sum
his munificence, who'd calm fire,
tax honor, Venus, hers, One he
      One begetter, and more is.

Which god, whose magic as almight-
y as put on a man and his love?
Whom call on, o men, whose magic's
heavenly? o Hymenaee Hymen,
　　o Hymen Hymenaee.

To youth's sighs tremulous parents
invoke you, to be yours virgin
zone loosens its little sinews,
timid man couples and he weighs
　　captive of his ear, married.

It's your fire in the young man's hands
flowers them with his girl's love, in-
deed she's your game you save from her
mother, o Hymenaee Hymen,
　　o Hymen Hymenaee.

Nil—potent? not even Venus,
fame of love, no bond, come probe it,
comes to convenience: yet potent
when only you will. Who's god to
　　compare here or who has it?

No law can assign that home, un-
blest by your newborn, no parent
stirps knit to the heir: yet potent
when only you will. Who's god to
　　compare here or who has it?

Why to this care rite is sacred!
no quota but yours presides o-
ver territories: yet quotas
when only you will. Who's god to
　　compare here or who has it?

Closed there, open it, Janus door,
virgin at hest! Won't you face in the
splendid tressed quaking of comets?
········· [lacuna MSS] ·········

274

tardy, ingenuous pure air:
.... [lacuna MSS] ....
when the mien makes out that it deigns,
    flawed, what tears, next she—is it?

flay your dewed sign now. No tear be, Au-
runculeia, peril cool, looms this—
no girl lovelier may descry
clear room, up, Ocean know day home
    with her, what went on and him.

Tall as in—various—so light—
wit his domine haughty, low—
star, o flows hyacinth in us.
Sad more worries, ah but day hastes:
    [prodigal, nova, nuptial.]

Prodigal, noval, nuptial, See,
hymn of her, yet how distant
now stray our words. Bride, heed the fires'
aureate tress quaking comets:
    prodigal, nova, nuptial.

No two ways' leave as in malice
dedicated adulterer,
probe-rut herpes pursuing queans—
ah his, *his* tenor is whole who'd
    sleep secure bare to your breasts,

leant to quick, well it at sight as
with ivy's implicate arbors,
implicate better in two one
complexion. Said ah but day hastes:
    bride, dye us, nova, nuptial.

O coo bill, lay, bed home imbues
.... [lacuna MSS] ....
....
....
    candid o bedstead leg to

quite two you win in one hero,
count all good they have, high wag ah
nightly, high mid day holiday—
good to that! Said ah but day hastes:
    bride, dye us, nova, nuptial.

Toll light ho! o pure kids' faces,
flame home the bride, veil, o now here!
In time conch sing in the mode, hymn
"io Hymen Hymenaee io,
    io Hymen Hymenaee."

Neigh, do, you, tuck it up, crow cocks,
Fescennine joke ah gait it o,
scatter nuts to pure boys *and get:*
desert him—domine weaned his
    quaint cute boy, noose on his arm.

The nuts to pure boys, no inners
quaint cute boy now: satisfied *then*
loose sistie, nook keep us: loop, bet
on, serve *here*, hear Talásio!
    Quaint cute boy, now scatter nuts!

Soared! they banned him the village cow,
quaint cute boy curried yesterday:
doomed too can shave at the barber's,
toned down his *me, sir ah me, sir*
    quaint cute boy, now it's the nuts.

The chorus may wail 'the *ah* 'tis
unguent, tight to the glabrous'—married,
abstain—you hear? I said abstain.
Io Hymen Hymenaee io,
    io Hymen Hymenaee.

Schemers hog tidbit—quite *licit*,
so long husband's not hog set: *married*
is to *know* not the same *licit*.
Io Hymen Hymenaee io,
    io Hymen Hymenaee.

And you too, go quick, girl, do as
you're petted, cavil nay and he goes—
petting *them* he'll wound you at that.
Io Hymen Hymenaee io,
    io Hymen Hymenaee.

End: to be home, his, with potence
that betides to virility,
why to be his and sharing that
(io Hymen Hymenaee io,
    io Hymen Hymenaee),

askew doom—trembling move on as
(can a tempest annihilate!)
the old whom home inbues nod to it.
Io Hymen Hymenaee io,
    io Hymen Hymenaee.

Transform all foreboding to good
clear the threshold, his Golden Foot,
rush alight, door, so be for him.
Io Hymen Hymenaee io,
    io Hymen Hymenaee.

Ah see into this occupant
of your bed, his Tyrian aura
total his immanence to be.
Io Hymen Hymenaee io,
    io Hymen Hymenaee.

He will not be minus nor you
picture your heart more intimate,
flame ahead his pent-in magic.
Io Hymen Hymenaee io,
    io Hymen Hymenaee.

Mite you, break from her little wrist,
pride in praetexta leave our girl:
hymn, coo, bill, lay, of her here—he.
Io Hymen Hymenaee io,
    io Hymen Hymenaee.

Old wives wed once but still their men's
one comfort in bed, benign women,
collocate here the little girl.
Io Hymen Hymenaee io,
    io Hymen Hymenaee.

Now's *licit* when *he* is, bridegroom,
how sure in love's bed move the best,
her eyes flowered light lightens as
all white parthenium—well it
    light to move, yellow poppy.

What married (ah tie me to Jove's
holy lights) lover no less love-
ly than she, no cue that Venus
neglected. Said a bit day hastes:
    pair, go! no ray more rare here!

Known, do you ray more at us, as
(home!) when *he's* boon ah to Venus
who worried, who'll hand him the palm,
what cup *his* capers have won him
    nothing absconds at the rim.

Will ay pulverize Africa,
seed a rum sky, make count a hum,
subdue cat numerous pries whose
quivers star—no more rare air—would
    mull the milliard loved way.

Loved to the belovèd, brief he
liberates that too: no, take it,
time—wet, his own line bear his
name, as is said *it was in them*,
    some pair, gain a forever.

Torquatus call your little boy,
mother's own greeting in his eye
poring, reaching tenderest hands,
all kiss riding it to father,
    semi-haunted baby smile.

Sit so, smiling like his father,
Manlius' facsimile incised,
nose cut that air of anyone knows
it, but the innocent looking eyes—
    mother's—indicate her: rare.

That all alluding to his good
mother laud his genius, approve,
call his unique air her hope of
him, reflect Telemachus meant
    fame for Penelope. O

close the doors, shut us out, virgins!
loose Muse satyrs! Good-bye now
young ones, be near living it up,
moon, air, ray ah see those valentines
    exercised in the young time.

62

Youths

Vesper out there, you vain knees can sure get up: Vesper, Olympus
expected all day, a wick's tending lumina tole it.
Sure see her come time us, come pink youths, linked choir rise
                                                    feasted,
come wined to the virgin, come dig the air *Hymenaeus.*

 Hymen o Hymenaee, Hymen it is o Hymenaee!

Girls

Care, it is in the *up! youths, vain knees?* Consort, girls, and counter:
nimb mere roam Oeta who is tended, Night afar ignites.
Seek air, test; we deign what pernickety exhilarated air?
no temerity exhilarates there, canon that we see is rarest.

 Hymen o Hymenaee, Hymen it is o Hymenaee!

Youths

No fickle ease no, boys, equals the palm, our parries' test:
ah speak of these unnipped girls seeking, meditating and requiring.
None frustrate meditate there, having memorably would see it,
no mere rune, pennate as with total mind they're laboring.
Not so all of our minds, all of us divided as our ears—
you're right to figure we wink more; *they* mate a victory to care.
Choir, reigning animus, salt them—committed to these throes;
they care and come in, keeping time, come respond here, echo a bit

    Hymen o Hymenaee, Hymen it is o Hymenaee!

Girls

Hesper, a quick wile o fares there crude daily or ignites?
keen Night time's posse's come, plucks a wailing girl from mother,
come, plucks a mother's own to nourish, her wailing girl in time,
yet the vain youth ardent you've cast him to own her, pure held lamb,
could enemy hosts cap it more crude or lie less uncurbed?

    Hymen o Hymenaee, Hymen it is o Hymenaee!

Youths

Hesper, a quick wile o—look you can die for joy—ignites?
keen star spun so to affirm his connubial flame, e-
quipped with the pride of the groom, promises, arrangements
                                  of parents,

nothing's contracted rite until you star extol it ardor.
Who'd doubt here all the Gods' felicity this optimum hour?

    Hymen o Hymenaee, Hymen it is o Hymenaee!

Girls

Hesperus, ai no boys, aie girls—was—he stole it—her name

. . . . [lacuna MSS] . . . .

Youths

Come now, your adventure's vigil is that custodian's ever—
knockabout lot, furies, whose hidden sighs revert nights to
Hesper—Who mutes you at dawn and apprehends as Eous.

[Hymen o Hymenaee, Hymen it is o Hymenaee!]

. . . . [lacuna MSS] . . . .

They love it, unnipped girls: fake tears, to carp—or a quest, who
quit whom? see carping, *tack it on him* meant they require *it*.

Hymen o Hymenaee, Hymen it is o Hymenaee!

Girls

What blossom's in sight sacred as nice obscurities,
ignored by cows grazing, not lain on, lost for the plough's rut—
winds mull it for hours, firm heat, sun a dew imbibes there

. . . . [lacuna MSS] . . . .

milling little pure boys like girls have hoped for a way there to play:
and then come to know the blossom deflowered with one finger,
newly illumined no boy or girl hopes for a way there to play:
seek where you go—intact, virgin meant home, care of the sweetest;
coom—when chastity missed—polluted core of the flower,
how could a pure boy enjoy that which meant no care to the girls.

Hymen o Hymenaee, Hymen it is o Hymenaee!

Youths

A widow on denuded ways, a vine not sure of harvest—
no home she can extol, no home it teems to make good wine—
say these untrained, prone, deflect as in a ponderous corpse
down, down continuing sum, the root decayed 'll flag them;
hankering farm rolling lads will not love her, not even the oxen.
Yet see where the vine twines the elm pole, conjunct in that marriage,

melting the willing farm lads mull into love's air, even the oxen:
seek where you go—intact, virgin meant home, not cult of senescence;
come par connubial mature time hour of the adeptest,
care and virile magic it means her man's zest least harms her parent.

[Hymen o Hymenaee, Hymen it is o Hymenaee!]

Don't be repugnant, come tally, conjugal, virgin.
Known, why act so pugnacious, father himself traded it—tipsy?
tipsy! father and mother? quibbles spar with necessity!
Virginity's known total's at least ex parte your parents;
tear it off part's father's, part is dated tear it off, mother,
the third is solely your taste: no lass would oppugn their two hopes
which go by right to the groom come into the dot—and you daren't!

Hymen o Hymenaee, Hymen it is o Hymenaee.

63

Spurred altering wake toss Attis his craft racing till marled in the
Phrygian wood—soon as his quick footsteps padded onto its earth
headed to the opaque silvas crest of the local deity—
stimulated as by infuriate rabies vaguest animus,
devolved his ill to acute flint spewing his ponderous testicles.
I take it relict *she* sensed her bit of membrane was not virile—
wet teeming rack and tare aie! soil sanguineous macula—and
he was *she* cut out to ape a woman's hands, love a typanum,
typanum, tuba Cybele's, to all, Mater, initiates,
tapping on skin once towering bull, tendering small cave to ten
                                                        digits—
canorous high sweet voice tasked trembling her band of committed
                                                        boys.
"Ah go to the high altar, Gallae, Cybele's None more rare, so mill
so mill onto Dindymus Mount domain of vague minds picked chorus,
alien here come patient willing exiles—look ah your lair, *here!*
set and my aim executed you came meek at my heel comates—
rapids, solemn to listing seas, truculent what could belay you,
white core castrated of Venus, her nimiety odious—
hail your true Hera—the hot tease, errant pulse of animate heart!
More at heart had meant decayed heart; so mill to me, singing many,

Phrygia our home Cybele's, Phrygian woods' None more rare to eye,
o be cymbal, loom sounded voice, o be tympana rebounded,
tibia can be, can it, freaks? curb woe, growl air, coll and mow,
o be capital Maenades' weighed jocking heads with their ivy crowns,
o be sacral sancta o hoot tease, ululant boys, agonize,
o be, sway with the Lady, high vaulting raring vaguest cohort:
who knows the cat's cut out is cool rare air to trip to these rites."
    So milling committed to Attis singing with not a male will
                                                     there—
thiasus' rap and a languishing of trembling tongue the boys ululate;
leeway—tympanum reechoed, cave—cymbal hollow, crepitant,
varied green skytossed wooded Ida prompts Her unimpeded chorus.
Fury bound, or so mill inhaling vaguely waded animus, against
comatose gasp tympana, Attis spurs a pack, no more, roar—ducks,
well, you'd think a young cow's wit shuns onus, indomitable yoke:
rabid aie! ducking, sicked on, under, Gallae probe ere *she* sped them.
They tack it home to Cybele; as they get there lassitude
numbs them all, a labored somnolence caps this hunt, no wine
                                            or Ceres.
Piggeries' lambent languor o cool eyes' sopor operate:
a bit in quiet mollifies rabid furor, animus.
So they'd be, err, He's aureate Sol, radiant imbues o cool eyes
luster white ethereal alba, solid earth here, marries sea foam,
depeopling a night's umbrage with a gait sounding of paced horses,
He bids Sleep's own exit and Attis wakens caught in what's about:
trembling waiting for him the goddess Pasithea receives Sleep's own.
It's then the quieted mulling ravaging sinewed rabies
which first so milled, spiked, tore at Attis, shows a fact, who'll
                                        recollect it,
liquid, how clear? mind tie with it? *she's no he*—a big cue for it,
animus hastening rushing ready tomb water led to it!
Here by marring and vast sea visions lachrymose mantling o cool eyes
path, tree, home, all locked to them, mist tossed high voice crying
                                        miserably.
    "Path tried father, o my country's trees, path, tree, home,
                    o mother begetting tree,
I have come to miss her relinquished: home! the meanest fugitive
                                          guile-
familiar insolent treads Ida, taught to lead no more than put feet
to a pood new snow hummed feral rheum gelid ah stable of frost, I'm
that I hear, am now all that they are, fury bound the lot pooling lairs,

I've been, am out keep; whose look's to stay, posit home, path, tree,
real or?
Coop, pit, deep set pupil of the eye sieves bids reads your dear air my
home,
robbed here afire how care reins doom, brief a tempest's animus
haste.
Agony! my how remote I hike faring in memory, my home,
path tree ah bone knees ah me kiss generate their ways, ah where o?
Ah where o forum, palaestra, stadium, that gymnasium?
Miss her I miss her—queer end doom's that I am, hot what! animate.
Quote any gain, whose figure has't, I go, unquote, hob to Her rim?
I'll go male all Her—I go adolescence, I go ephebus, I go pure boy,
I go gymnast, was fluffy as floss, I go rubbed, decked as with olive,
me-he, Januses frequented, me-he, liminal tepidness,
me-he, flowered wreaths, corollas redeemed the home I'd inherit,
linking then as it might be Heart to, me-he, Sol in my cubicle.
Eh go, handmaiden, minister to Cybele's family, farer?
I go Maenad, I go me-apart, I go where sterile is hero?
I go, virid is algid, Ida—no way to make that look like home?
I go with time a game, sob altered, Phrygian columbaria,
to be cared for silva cult deer, to be a boar's memories' vague gust?
I'm, I'm doled out agony, I'm, I'm whipped penitent."
Rosy his (what cheek!) little lips, sound tossed—whose?
skittish so be it,
geminate ears of the gods are raised, annunciate a reference,
unbinds juncture of yoke, resolved and Cybele looses her lion-boys,
livening quick core of a host, the left lion, with a lance, Look at Her!
"Ah get him!" and chants "ah go, Fierce eye, fag that hunk, furor
agitate
facture of furors so thick the mad return no more from my forest,
may he live harried here, numb his imperious cupidity.
Ah go, cut out! tear your cat hide! tail reverberating patter!
fast hunkers moving into your frame, toll! call! roar! intone!
rut you! lam! fire rocks to rose the curve of neck quaking your mane."
Aie it hikes, mean ax! Cybele relegating the yoke to hand.
Fierce the beast sways, tears off to his haunts' rabid doom incited
animus,
wandered frenzied ringing rived where the gilt feet pad vague on—
out, up by humid alba of sands, looking glitters, the sea's at it,
then a turn and caught feeble Attis probed by marmoreal plashed sea,
attacked him, the demented fleeing forever into the forest:

to be ever no man but the spayed woman familiar fleeing.

Deign ah magnificent Cybele, deign in your domain Dindymus,
proclaim ah my goodness such furious madness far from my home:
all of those, ah go inciting those, all those who go robbed of *those*.

64

Pelion could one time prong its top worthy keel in pines
ancestor lugged clear to Neptune in his sea purr on thus
to Phasis what flood tides on the fees of Aeetes,
came elect young ones ace, Argive eye robe awry pubes,
aureate time hoped on there's Colchis afar to raid pelt home,
asea soon what deep salt sough hit at the careerer poop in
cerulean currents abeyant knees a fir oar palm ease;
Divine Goddess retaining on summits orbs of her fortress
inspired levity made 't volitant hum flaming wind courier,
pinewood conjoint gains in flexed keel text a careening.

Wild sea mull ache rose throe wind tossing prow scudded ichor,
turned on the rowing oar spume wisp in canted wave under,
emerge serry fret the candent way gurgle of welters
a choir who eye moonstruck—Nereides admire Wonders.
I'll lay that who'll lay odds we daren't, lucky marine eyes
mortal ace o cool lease knew that day corporal Nymph eyes
new trick tiniest extant as who gurgled there can know.
T' my Thetis this Peleus incandesced fair thru his armor,
t' my Thetis human knows none despised hymeneals,
t' my Thetis the Father Himself would join them Peleus sense it.
O names that I hope to, sage lore whom time bore then happy
heroes aye salvé, the Gods' own gens, o benign mothers,
progenies aye salvé to you in turn salvé the benign arm,
voice go so I pay my own voice harmony compel I bōw:
take it how dear your song sings in me tide days felicitous pine torch,
Thessaly aye column man Peleus, you whom Jupiter Himself,
Himself so chose Divine Genitor conceded a marriage.
Did not Thetis twine you what, pool care rim on—Nereus' heir then?
Did not sublime Tethys consent that granddaughter nap then,
Okeanos choir *marry* totalling ample clasp of our orb home?

Wish small o hoped hour infinite time poring look who's
at their wedding, domain convening all who frequented
Thessaly, a palace there light and the ray of the courted:

donors faring presents, declared in gold and in virtue.
Deserted their Cieros—link once to Phthiotica Tempe,
Crannon is Quiet Homes—and moat and wall of Larissa,
Pharsalian cohort, Pharsalia takes to frequént haunt.
Rural clod is no more, molesting collars yoke no steers,
none humbles or clears his poor garden vine with a rake's thrusts,
none flails at thinning out fronded tall row or arbors' umbrage,
none glebe bound prove one old bull dragged earth here and tore it,
squalid a desert's ruby gone in for rust ploughs a rot trees.

    I see his Seat, say this, honeycomb opulent aisle recesses
ranging on, fulgent and splendent aureate and argent hall.
Candid ivory solely ease, goblets light pour cooly men sigh
to the home whose good wit regales a splendid eye gazing.
Look now where Her Own Divine nuptial bed will glow on their
State abodes in midway ease, Indic white elephantine tooth
tinct with coveted rose of conchylium purple spread—full glow:
    a tapestry's pristine men a variety of figures
heroes who mirror virtues such indicate art there.
Name her fluent sounding shore prospect thence leave her at Dia
Theseus gone on then clear out sea comb ah clash to endure
untamable's the torn heart carries Ariadna's furors,
not doomed yet in time see see what she will see sear her crave it,
would but a false lagging ache that she dream harks back to doze,
                                        no—
désert inconsolable misery sand care not arraign her.
A memory youth won his fugitive blade plights water remiss,
heard with the wind toss sigh link wanes promise he broke he'll lie.
    And from coiling alga mice tease Minoïs' welling eyes
as ax had hewed effigy as Bacchante's proves stone speaks, *ēbĕu*,
proves stone speaks, wet margins her, roar roam fluctuate one dies,
no yellow hair retains subtly her fair circlet midcrown,
no chiton to lave a veil at her breast eyes are moved to,
none tear at the striving laced in elegance of her nipples,
all one ah wild thought too collapses a corporeal passing
into seas haunting her feet flows salt sallies hallooed outbound.
So no care to mere tress no care to fluid antics that mix clothes,
a life wink in currents, thought as you'd expect tore her, Theseus,
thought torn and no more, thought *you* penned day bot paired her
                                       demented.
Ah misery, assiduous qualm look the bruise waxed waned of wit

spinose seeds Erycina's sirens a pack tore her care as
in lulling tempest that day, fair as cold, time bore her Theseus
across seas, courage will lead horde way past Piraeus
out to get injustice Ruler's Gortynian temple.

Now peer bent in old time gruelling pest a God hacked them
Androgeos' agony pain must absolve their killings
elect host youths winsomely led the girls who'd not know their arms
Cecropia's holy time issue that fed the roaring Minotaur.
Which anguished (ah malice combs mean when old walls wear under)
even the same Theseus' procreant care for his Athens
probed asked for death but his choice rather than tally his Cretan
funerals, Cecropian funerals portage that rent her,
and cutting the waves leeward knee tense whack lenient hush arrives—
"magnanimous" odd Minos o vain its Seat once called "superb" *base.*
One small look and cupid o come speaks it lumined a virgin
regal all qualm suavest expiring chastest odors
little girl's in mulling compassion mother's her little bed
gales as Eurotas proves bringing flume onto myrtles
air ave distinct as it'd talk with all vernal colors,
no, preeing his will glowed flagrant there would decline no whit
lumined eye, qualm caught up in one corporeal flame and
wounded thus what squeamish ache sears it tears at her marrows.
Hĕŭ Misery exacting His immitigable Heart's furors
Sacred Boy your cares of men mean and good God how you mix
these, why quiz Her of Golgi why quiz Idalium frond O Sum,
quail abyss incénse ah crack tease her mind poor little one
flutter in his yellow strands pity hostage sighs peer into him!
Want crush ill at heart lit languishing cored out timorous!
Want turned sigh pain mocks her fulgor such pale yellowed aura,
can see him coping hence contrive contend with their monster
'outmode him or better death, Theseus, outpride him may lower *this.*'
None ingrate tho They may frustrate, moon as cool Deities,
promised thence tacit o kindled íncense vows lips below.
Now will it in sum o! craunching mountain branches of Taurus'
great oak or coniferous sweating torn cortex of pine down,
indomitable wind contorts it as flame might roar by
a root until pulling up all covered roots extirpates earth
prone and *had it,* lot a crash hugged conquest all the way fragments,
sick dominated savage prostrate corrupt horror, Theseus
now quicked only its vain tossing of horns on the winds.
And then pedate safe pace multiplying laud reflects it

errorabounding regions tenuous thread guiding him feeling
noil labyrinth's haze of flecks high walls a gradient timed
tactile whose forest might turn inobservably his error.
   Said quit I go on primal digressions harmony plural
commemorate, what link wanes genitor is failing 'ah would whom'
'what's *consanguine* sister come bless me, what *denying* mother,'
'why misery m'own daughter departed there light head,'
only his, his, Theseus' told him bride her rite what more then,
out would wake the raft his, spume a soused litter at Dia,
out on his arm mull lee then winking lumina sleep—no
liquor it in memory absconder's pectoral conscience?
Sigh plying wail probed often ardent her heart dire fury teemed
clarisonous emerged feud asea a pack tore her voices
hacked up precipice tryst him conn scan there the mountains,
on to eye comb implacably vast those—pretend there at—iced whose,
tomb tremulous sallies adverse salt broke hurry her in and douse
mull her leg nudity toll antagonize her *sure* eye,
what cry *in extremis* might stem death's wish say quarrels, is
frigid or lost utters single tears o racked cóntent.
   "See can you my path betrays how weak torn, perfidy, father's
                                                             hearths
perfidy, deserted I linger how little recked, Theseus?
See can you discard hence neglect our numina devious
in memory, devoted homing—perjuries are portals?
Null honor is part of wit crude a least fleck there a means to
counseling one? to be null after you'd claim me at a price tho,
who meted it knows trust wells with misery's care and pities?
Ah not those quondam bland high promises your deeds in-
voked in me hear, nothing, misery spare her your hope babbles,
said *connubial light* then, said *hope to those*, hymeneals:
quick hunted aërial díscard point here it it went here.
Harm! harm no love or oath—he'll rant and woman accredit
no love weary spirit serve man as he see sieved faithless;
his doom a licked greed coupling his animus progs questing
                                                          apace keen
he'll mate one to adjure her and he'll promise her there, parched
                                                                 hunt:
so th' sooner cupidity mind is satiate and lives its lust,
dicta nor he'll matter or fear, no will perjuries are current.
Cared to go to you then mid the o whirr sund'ring turbulent
                                                            late death

I rescued you, and put aside gored my own my own brother, craven!
and to be failing here supreme o in temper—I the same;
broken the like a randy fiercest boar and alighting birds' squeak
pride, and no kin who hacked at my tomb who labor more to unbury.
What dam to gender you so lost the rock whelped lioness?
cold marrow conceiving spume wanting waves' cesspit spewed undies,
why Syrtis, why Scylla rape ax, why vast ah Charybdis,
tally ah queer redress prodigal prime I invited?
Say to be known *your dear* were errant, could not be (one knows true
scion's cold horror bides pristine precept his parents teach)
yet to mean in his trust but a least tear 'do care I say this,
how'd it be you come tho formally our servant' love borne ah
candid I'd pour lucent liquids wash white his toes and limbs, ease
purple forever turn down count stars in vesture could bed live.
        Say't quickly go who ignores unquickened conqueror airs, it's
I stir now to malice, why no least sense imbues outcry,
next misses aught, hear their quiet never returned voices?
He'll lay out then proper you madding hiss vast ardor unwound waves,
next wish come apart, what vacua mortal is in alga.
Sickness and insults extreme of time poring savage
force eat into these straws envy dead questions hush our ears.
        Jupiter Omnipotence would no night had ever borne him to
Gnosus Cecropian tethering his fleet to our coast, peace
undermined year to year offerings stuffed into our Minotaur,
Perfidy's in Crete his relegated navy a funeral
neck male he's villainous tool kiss cruel lying formal
conciliating: traitress relinquished that Seat with its hospice!
Now who may reverence? How lease hope peered-at death neater?
Idomeneus' parent mountains? Ah gurge in the litter
discord hence pounding truculent sea divided the gods' ichor?
And father's anxiety spare me? whom now, myself, relinquish,
raised spurious youth's venom fraught her own kind a secure death?
Can I guess at faith or console I may meet my lover
when he forgot love in those scurrying oars without remorse?
Pride tearing and no love light us, soul and no soul protect you,
now parted a grave sea's plighting him King in the waves undoes:
new life forgot rotted o new love's hopes, o mean and mute here
all meaner sound desért here, ostent in death o mean late tomb.
Known to my end teem in me languish scant lumina mortal
new Prayer as I face so sick the end corporal senses,
qualm Justice and Wisdom expose come prove that hate wilt him,

Guileless Dooming feed me past raving come pray care an hour.
　　Harrow fated virulent taunting vindictive, pain ah
Eumenides, keen whose snake anguished crowns wreathed in your hair
　　　　　　　　　　　　　　　　　　　　　　　　　　billow,
frenzies expiring breaths preordained packed hearts and ires,
hook hook on to me till my cries are heeded, querulous,
waste I go aie misery the streams which pour from my heart dull wails
go goring hopes, ardent eyes madden cark and fear horror.
Quick on my way right, now sundered, the truth deep in me,
wish no love I part with, no sorrow vanished, scour look Doom!
seethe call him *desolate* Theseus my mind too relinquished,
till he lament there, dire Furies, sick himself and his kind."
　　As past qualm moans stopped poured forth tear by tear of her
　　　　　　　　　　　　　　　　　　　　　　　　　　cares
supplicating sigh wished *expose* (skeins) anxious—the fact is
He nodded, invoked *He* Guileless One knew and Heaven roared,
come out to tell us what with Earth riding countermove tremor round
a choiring ocean concussive mica count sidereal mundane.
Asea out there cark a mind tho calling on nothing Theseus
(conceit's oblivious, dim is it pecked at or conquered?)
what mandate had previously turned round in his mind *that*
too clean left him, he missed extolling his signal entry
suspecting Erechtheus' sad hopes dared dream would see her hero
　　　　　　　　　　　　　　　　　　　　　　　　　　home.
　　Now we've heard when the line sailed from the mole of Athene
(linked and then nothing, wind one's son would credit) Aegeus
to delay clasped his young son and by way of mandate said this:
　　"Not in me I long ah who could not dear one equal the day
redeemed you to me, grace I knew not meant for my sentence
　　　　　　　　　　　　　　　　　　　　　　　　　　of years,
not I who go calm in dubious courage dim with the air of causes,
quandary condemning fortune make me act and you have fervid
　　　　　　　　　　　　　　　　　　　　　　　　　　virtues
separating from me tho I die, who will long until my known doom
look on me, son, knotted care who sighed for your face and your eyes:
no I cannot goad hence lightly my heart tormenting me,
nor try ferret son your fortune, her signal *she can't die*,
sad brimful mulled housed heart promise meant yet querulous
can I do other my gray hairs than defile pour dust on my head;
in the fateful hour you go hang these dark sails on the mast love,
untrusted luckless truststriking enkindlings our minds tease,

canvases obscure hallowed lot of rust blueing Iberia.
Grant it be She sancta consecrated in holy Itonus,
whose trust in our gens accedes to defend her Erechtheus,
honor us, spurt your right hand with the sinning Bull's bloodstream,
turn for the fact to Her let memory deepened conned in your heart
                                                  then
act to honor our mandate, let no lapse obliterate this:
that sailing back to us when your eyes son loom on our hills
you must stop mourning then, strip down your rigging, divest the
yardarms of black, run up the halyard one white sail, rue vanish
when proof then discerns such light and good in my mind and
knows who's come home to render my old age prosperous in state."
    Heard th' old man and promised, constant yet his mind went
                                             from him,
Theseus cooled, pulse of a wind flummery nubilous
aeriform new falling mountain snow leaking the bare summit.
The father, who'd sum all prospect then from the lookout, perturbed
anxious ah assiduous consuming luminous flayed dews
comprehending only a wind swelling glint of black sail,
precipitant see! see! hurls himself from the verge *that craggy height!*
ah missing credence imitate Theseus' fate, die!
Sick funest that home whose son's greeting's death of a father—
more than heroic Theseus quailing Minos' daughter looked to,
obliterated mind now memory that learned its sin would grieve it.
Look once again at the cadent masthead careening home
multiplicate animus voluble sough keel of her cares.

    A part of the coverlet flowerings whirled about Iaachus
come thiasus Satyr roar and Nysa gens of Silenus,
they choir *hence, Ariadna, take her away incénse our mad loves.*

. . . . [lacuna MSS] . . . .

whipped alacrities passing lymph wild demented fury *band*
evoe Bacchantes evoe come bŏw them and flecked heads daze.

    Ha room! pace tack tack cavort the bound cuspid of thyrsus,
pass aie divulge o jocund bounced members you want cow,
pace see see tortures serpentine twistings cincture, bound
pass into obscure caves celebrating orgies in caskets,
orgies ah that frustrate cupidity dare not profane here;
plangent band ah lift high rake timbrels, cymbal and palms beat
out aery thing the newest thinning tune's airy copper bound—

mules these raucous sound nose a flybynight horn how pompous—
barbaric horrible lilling strident but tibia cant too.
  All of these exemplary virtues decorated the figures
pulled over as pledge to smooth the nuptial bed amid state.
As the curious stares of standing Thessalian youths
explained it sanctities bid they cede their eyes to th' Gods'.
Here whiles as float a placid sea mar—a matutinal
hurry roughens, Zephyrus' proclivities kindling to douse
Aurora yet oriented vague if subliminally Sol's,
while tardy prim a clement wind flame in a pulse aie
proceed then, levities queer sonant plangent roar cachinnate,
post wind o crescendo makes it makes it increasingly
purple arcing proclaims now it is by what look refulgent,
so ebb the guests a while still linked by ties of the regal court
as they crisscross vaguely pass on their way rayed who disband.
  Coming first after them Princely Keeper of Pelion—
advent of Chiron brought down thru his trees their donor:
name what so quicked grows in its plains, or Thessaly's mighty
mountainous auras create, such propped hardy flowers flumes dance
hourly ah pare it flowers tepid with fecund Favonius,
how indistinct each plexus he lit his sept corollas,
whose blossoms glad a home's jocund o risible odor.
Fast by him Penëus at hest from the green haunt of Tempe—
Tempe Vale's sylva cinctured superimpendent trees,
Minosim linked hands Doris celebrant dance in chorus—
not without gifts: now come into light uprooted trees, exalt tall
beeches, erectile procreates stipitate laurels,
nor 's he now without nodding plane tree, lenitive sister of
flame entombed Phaëton, his poplar, aery cypresses.
He circled the Seat plaiting a text for the lovèd,
vesting ambulatory velvety frond ever green writ.
Posting in his footsteps solitary hearted Prometheus,
extenuated grievance worn out trace vestige of pain o-
vercome once he learned to restrict limbs to rock, cut chained ah
but resolved pendant of lost vertical precipice.
Indeed th' Father had now come, sanctioned Heaven's Queen and
                                            their sons to
the wedded—that left you alone, Phoebus, along with
your own twin sister dwellers on the mountains of Idrus:
Peleus—*can't take him,* paired to your sister who spurned him as

she did Thetis—*torches? let who will celebrate her crude nuptials.*
 Th' Gods who'd come, ivories relaxed them, curled on seats,
artless

largely occupied with horns of plenty deep-piled viands,
in the interim the infirm quaking ancients, corporal motile
verity's host Parcae grouped around, aired incantations.
Each corpus tremulous completely under white vestment
shining with purple edge at the ankles, each cincture of aura,
what rose on a new snow o resided in white hair or headband,
eternally their hands carried on a ritual labor.
Left hand holding distaff and wool retained on it (ah mixture)
dexter hand will levitate take down these threads (feels *up* in these
formed about digitals) thumb pronate 'down' policy torque wanes
liberate the spindle whorl 's about round in now fusing,
and what threat they cure pain 's about smoothed bitten off with their
teeth,

wool ends as of arid locks of hair abound morsels on bit lips,
what previously would furl on the thread extant if a lull:
at their feet always near candescent more light than wool white
rolls of fleece well guarded custom bound small willow baskets.
Hike t'whom clarisonous pelting the rolls of fleece, voiced then
the tale ah divinely poured from them harmony Fate their
harmony, perfidy could in no late time argue its heart.

Honor his excellence, magnanimity, virtues your gains,
Emathia, to your men powers, clear 's the fame of your son,
ah keep the good light of today span we looked into—Sisters'
wayridden true oracle. Said once, why Fate has to sing under,
 hurry the skeins and the spinning and ah hurry what few see.

Advent and yet to be, come portent and hope to th' married here
Hesperus, advent and yet wish to come, star in their conscience,
how 't will be flows on in her meant him pour forth love and
more love
languidly who's closer by it take him into your young slumbers,
lave ah sustaining arms his robust neck your column.
 Hurry the skeins and the spinning and ah hurry what few see.

No loves' home has told us weaving on one text of lovers
no loves have more to tell conjoin seek further rayed mandates

while all that is is Thetis, all is concord with her Peleus.
　　Hurry the skeins and the spinning and ah hurry what few see.

Now seed your own blood's fearless of terrors Achilles,
host of foes, how to go? set forth if breast torn no truce,
quick pass by peer why *go* victor certain win his coursers
flaming outferret th' deer gale ere his vestige will care why.
　　Hurry the skeins and the spinning and ah hurry what few see.

None who'll quest war'll bellow he compares with this hero,
come Phrygian Teucrian man in one sanguine river,
Troy crashing walls sift down longing call turmoil and bellow
perjurer Pelops lay waste to it—the third of his heirs.
　　Hurry the skeins and the spinning and ah hurry what few see.

He will with his excellent virtues such clarified acts as
cipher Fate bring to their dead sons funereal mothers,
come uncoiling long hair sobbing ah averted crowned gray
putrid at heart infirm as they rave and beat old breasts with
　　　　　　　　　　　　　　　　　　　their palms.
　　Hurry the skeins and the spinning and ah hurry what few see.

Now come will it dense as ripe crops of corn th' farmer harvests
sunlight so ardent of yellow flame demitted arable:
Troy's young mown down with foe's steel prostrate and corpses
　　　　　　　　　　　　　　　　　　　in furrow.
　　Hurry the skeins and the spinning and ah hurry what few see.

Test his air earth mog knees virtue to be 's under Scamander,
what passing rapid o diffused into Hellespont o
who is in the crush sees anguished slain corpses in great heaps
altered to deep tepefied purr mixture of blood and cold tide.
　　Hurry the skeins and the spinning and ah hurry what few see.

. . . . [lacuna MSS] . . . .

Then ache cue test his air earth mortal booty ready to pride ah
coom earth's ash excels so cumbustible heap round barrow burns now
she is given as new white snow pierced corpse by him virgin odd
　　　　　　　　　　　　　　　　　　　truce.
　　Hurry the skeins and the spinning and ah hurry what few see.

Name simulacra fagged deed dared Fortune's *come on* Achaeans
your bid 's Dardania her Neptune's own dissolving link wall,
(all told!) Polyxenia made of we win blood for sepulcher,
aie will it and cut two-edged succumb head victim of error,
broken headless trunk submits so poppled knee corpse pus.
     Hurry the skeins and the spinning and ah hurry what few see.

Quarry ah go to your hoped host animate conjunction of lovers.
Ah keep that goddess, man, felicity faith of her, dear one,
do deed her, Cupid, to him do do nuptial marry them.
     Hurry the skeins and the spinning and ah hurry what few see.

Nor will her nurse tricks of the rising sun looking in sense
yesterday, collar for her neck now too small for her love,
nor anxious nag mother, discord's mist on a puling girl
sigh the bride lies alone despair ever of little ones.
     Hurry the skeins and the spinning and ah hurry what few see.

     Tally all prophecies one time felicity hailed Peleus
harmony divinely chanted from the breasts of the Parcae.
Presences Gods came once to visit the homes of the pious,
heroes might yet see mortal and gods stand there together—
godly call high no man would spurn piety his holy bond.
Saw Father of the Gods temple refulgent revisit His
annual Kalends feast venerated sacrifices he'd
come to see on earth count then by hundred prone taurine.
Saw Bacchus as Liber, Parnassus' vertigo summon
Thyades effuse his *hey on* tease crinite heads *ay get,*
'come Delphic townsfolk hurl toward him exuberance routings,
ah keep Your Own Light here Dear God fume mount! busy altars.'
Siding in lethal war o beleaguered town 'Ah mien of Mavors!
out rapid heed Triton's own daughter! out Rhamnusian virgin!'
armored as men whom god's presence exhorted to courage.
Said past come tell us sclerous crime imbued earth, men founder,
justice has gone and always cupidity and mind figure ground,
perfidy on their hands brothers now strangle their brothers,
destitute extinct those sons who looked after their parents,
mourned them, but today's father primps at junior's funeral
libertine impatience bother to deflower his new mother,
innocent martyr son steered to impious incest,
impious no fear or taste divines scald wrath of her parent gods:

all law once founded unfounded malice a mixture of furor
justifying no blest mind may await gods' ray where or home.
Where there are no tales dignifying Their Ways They cut us,
nor seek contingent patient touch to illumine clear air.

65

Yet see (may as I do) a confect of my cure—a dolor
     say woke ah that docked these, Hortalie, Virgin new bays
(neck poet's ash, dull kiss Muse our room)—ex-pro merry Fate use
     men's animate haunt as fluctuate dips of malice:—
now am come here new, pair Lethe's gurge, my dead brother's
     pallid foot, luminous hauled under appear dim,
Troyan Rhoeteum whelm him, sob, tear, litter tell us
     a wrapped tomb knows trees, brother, with racked looks of leaves.

.... [lacuna MSS] ....

[hollo, where? how dear air o numb qualm to a fact all locked
                                        in them]
     numb qualm I go to wait death, brother, I my beloved or
I speak who am—post, hock. What care, the same pair, ah *my* boy,
     same pair, my state too, your—harmony more toll cannot
quell aie a sob dense as rumoring cone kin to the breeze,
     Daulias assumed by Fate again mourns Itylus:—
sad time when intent is my brother's loss, Hortale, might I
     hack, express a bit of harmony—Battiades',
not to addict a vague guess and become credit to the winds,
     off looks which say my effort to put these on's no more;
remiss I'm spun see, furtive, or moon air or apple,
     procure it chaste o virgin as a green girl who
would (misery!) believe the apple her breast looked out to,
     whom, (odd) when her mother proved she lied, her secret out:
to weigh, elude (prone—no precepts) agitate her course, she
     who quicks man and tryst is conscious of a ray rue bore.

66

Human all key mog knee this pecks it loom in a moon the
 key stellar room mortice—comb pare it outweigh obit as
flame may use what rapid day Sol is knit or obscure ray tour,
 hood cadent curt this sidereal time pore of us,
hood Trivia forth t'him sub Latmus sexed her ray elegance
 t'who'll kiss her—moon—gear o day woke it ah airy o—
he then whom I hail Conon celestial in enlumined wit *did*
 eye Berenice's lock vertigo's skies' hair I am—
full—gain teem clear ray, I'm all this lady dear her arm
 laid vowing, prodding bright goddesses, polled lock in taste,
qua rex tempest hothead new vow act his hymeneal—
 waste stating *finis* of all rat Assyrians—
dual key a nocturnal portance vestigial ricks eye,
 qualm the virgin, he is *guess her right* exudes with his.
Has no novice upped ease O dear o Venus, outwitted parent, doomed
 frustrate heir—false sees gowdie a lachrymal lees,
o bedroom tell me, was she intraliminal fountain?
 No, I tell my diva, for all you moaned, you weren't.
That my lady mulled—tease! talk of wit reigning, a querulous
 in in seeing her vowed prowler off the war hero.
Ah two none orb whom looks tee—deserted coo bill lay—
 said frayed risks carry flay belay the scathed home:
qualm pent in whose moist eyes exceeded cure or middle ways!
 You to bid him total pectoral solicitude!
sense—abuse, a rape, tease—mind excided! had to go, care to
 cog, know him—apart once virgin and magnanimous.
And had by now obliquitous fogginess corralled my queen—adept
 whose
 cunning won a king, when for his cause you sought all eyes?
Sad too misty for him—he thence—wail, farewell look you tossed!
 Jupiter, what wrested luminous eye wipe manner!
Quiz the mute Godhead taunted you thus? And could a man tease
 known longing from care, her poured body at best will its end?
At will bid me become this—prodigal conjurer, divi-
 sive '*see now* towering on sanguine bull's holocaust,
see red'—with Whom you elicit. His hounding temper ere long holds
 captive Asia, Egypt to finite ways added her right.
Whiz I go pro fact this coil hasty readied to cut to
 pristine (a woe to know woe) moon hurry this soul you owe.

A withe ah, o regnant head, to all the vertigo, sky, see—
　　a withe ah: adjure you dear head who keep me put to it,
dig him for rot who'd seek his in on it ere what air you are at:
　　sad withe tho severed postulate it is iron?
It laid quaking averse such mountain, whence maximum in auras
　　progeny of Thia clears a superway hither,
came Mede tempering iron no womb married—comber you went as
　　permeant clastic—barbarous knifed it Athon.
Quit fogging crinkly hairs, if iron tally high cut down?
　　Jupiter! would Chalybes all men of that vain race rot,
wet key prinked hip with o sapped tare earth harrower vain as
　　instated slag, iron stringer endured heat of him!
Abject, I polled lock and the comae my ah fated sorrowers,
　　look, unbound! comes see Memnon's (who's Ethiopia's)
unijugate (impel lanes) nutant imbues aery pennons,
　　up too lit Arsinoe's Locris' ostrich lashing horse,
he scampers aether, he has me to lanes, of all light embrace
　　what Venus risk has to collocate in gremial.
It's She saw him—Zephyritis—her own famulus league her rite,
　　Greek at Canopus—incolant—littoral—views.
And there Venus varies o one solemn and illumined sky, lea-
　　guers us Ariadne's aureate time, pairing us
(fix a crown off her forehead) said now's your queue, full gay ray, most
　　devoted, flower where the scissors kiss you away,
you whittle on, ah flayed to cadent in my temple—there I may
　　see dews in antique stars—the wan new one opposite:
Virgo in whose sigh we count the gains—angry Leonis
　　lumina, Callisto young to Lycaon—when I
wear, turn in accosting, herding (doused) on to Boötes,
　　he wakes unhurried all night to merge into Ocean.
Say't qualm, qualm may nightly preen me, vestigial gods doom,
　　lights out day, can I, Tethys, yield, *rest it*—to wit,
(peace to your ire for I ache like I hate, Rhamnusian virgin,
　　now can I go on a lie, fear all the more to what gain,
not seeming infests these serpent sidereal dictates,
　　candid, o queen, veritable hours'll will you I am):
none as time light or ray hues, who may offer as whimper,
　　offer ah me, atone my own—vertigo disgracing her—
quick come ago, t'whom, virgin, one then fiat, many ways dispersed
　　unguents, these in a millifold melt imbibing.

You girls who hope to come young to luminous tidings,
    don't press to union amiss, corporal cunning husbands
treading in nudities, reject your vests peeping nipples;
    calm with unguent dab me—my honor, lidded onyx,
vest, store onyx—cast o holy ties adjuring nubile law.
    Sad case who's impure o deeded to adultery,
ill her use ah, may light dust not leave unimbibed irritable wisps:
    no I can't go indignities, prime me ah no life's petty.
Said *mog* as—o new brides—some pair concord there a way stirs—
    some pair, are more, say days and call love assiduous.
To where, o regnant head, to whence come these stars, divine
    placebos festive lumina whose Venus reigns—
unguents, see you spur them, don't sever these as once turned
                                       from me,
    set by the eyes largess, offering my honor imbues.
See stars curry, retain me? I'm torn from a queen's regal hair, famish:
    proximous Hydrochoi full go rating Orion!

67

O dear cool you couldn't a virile—you couldn't a parent he—
    salvé! take weigh bone ah Jupiter act it open,
Janus, door! when Balbo thickened—serviced his benignant
    ol' him—home say days hipped seized say next tenure heat—
how come fare runt hearsays 'n how the door serve very malignly
    posthumous poor wrecked torn father's young married son—eh.
Decode it dumb no-beast, choir a moot hot affair, how is
    in dome and numb veteran deserved service unfit him?
"No (not that—Caecilius, placate him, who we trot it to and some)
    culpableness, calm calm thicket tour is who me—ha,
neck peck at whom ha—me, quiz calm potent thicker a quick qualm:
    worm mistiest populace yarns *you door, quit, you fog it;*
queer—quack come quail all liquid (repair, a tour) non-benefactor—
    odd me, human's clamant: *ya knew, door, culprit thou wast.*"
Known is to sate a zest, *you* know to dicker away bo,
    said *fog*, you riot, quibbles scenting at what we diet.
"We possum? No man queried nor scored our labor, what?"
    Nose wall, you must: no peace dickerer neigh do, bit, talk.
"Pre-mum echoed your *virgin* (quote) fared here, trod it ah no bis—
    false: sums't. No, a lame heir pre-erred how to go right,

languid—ee—or tenderer cue wee pendant sickly-like beet, a
  noon qualm say made him so as two lit odd tunic come:
said father he loosed his gnat's wife, he laced his son's coo bill lay—
  thicket their misery and conscience sclerotic home hum;
say we quote 'impious man's blind core flogged rabbit the more' or
  say you quote 'he nurtured sterile semen in his son as a rot,
requiring thus his own do for the nervous issue's ill load,'
  quote 'pa said, son, I'm sole for your virgin and home'."
A great game (it narrows) mirror of piety—parent (hm . . .)
  quips his son's wee, knot and minx, her it—in (grim ahem . . .).
"That quean now solely hoax 's a dig't hot cognate hum up in rare
  Brixia, Chinea's up a site, two specula,
flows its calm yellow—purr, current, flume and—the Melo,
  Brixia, Verona's mother, ah my tie, my eye;
it's said Postumius and Cornelius now rate her more and
  come quip bouse, ill love mulling, fake at adultery—whom—"
Is this right, caller 'll quiz: "what! you who's stuck, on'y a door,
                                                  knows this?
  who can't come from domain of the liminal, at best lick it,
no populace auscultator, setting so fixed to a lintel,
  tightened offer here a soul is out, or appear open—*home?*"
"Sigh plying out of her, furtive a vocal low quaint time,
  sole confidantes sleek girls hike 's oo ah *flagitious*, and
naming their thick intimates dixit must, would hope that qua me
  spare a right neck, lingua, as see! I've no ear to cull 'em.
Pride overheard, added *but quondam when*—dicker, eh? no I'll
  nominate none to light rube red super cilia:
long as a mast man was accused—litigants onto the limb,
  false, a mean dock!—of ventral puerperium."

68

Cold how mean, fortune consuming you oppresses your care, your
  kind script would look lachrymose, mists in this little letter—
now fragmented ejecting spume man the waves *ai* Korè was in this—
  sob, lave what mortalities lean on me—restitute him,
whom no sancta of Venus may leave rest or sleep, heir to his now
  deserted bed, a love called away perpetual,
nor weather him old songs the poets harmony, Muses
  all blacked out, come—mind's anxious and purview views late;

it greets me, me he makes one with him, to be the cares say my own,
    'my need rocks for that Muse around, your petals and Venus—
                                              rites':
sad, to your need my own says I know I too've come to that, Manli,
    knowing me would it be easy to put off an old friend,
how keep up, submersed as fortune now flouts its waves, asea—
    no, I am lost—and miseries deny me the gifts you ask.
Time poured there white, my prime vested me, I trod out the purest—
    who counted, come of state, flowers that spring air carried,
multitudes loose, serious? known as the Goddess knew us, knows that
    care will come, cures with mixed sweet a marred bitter time:
sad—a tomb, heart that stood me, looked to—fritter in me remorse
    that stole it. O misery brother your death ends it for me,
to me without you remains this fragment come to earth brother—
    take him and now waste us—our tree's split—pull down the house,
o now we are taken and none part in ruin, go down as our tree,
    gone to us and with a kiss, had you lived I'd love more.
Because you go inter here too all that I meant here forever,
    all study that aches in all men, that delights see animate.
Caring your script bids "Verona's torpor, Catullus,
    as here what whack's wall-squeezed day, male high, lords with no
                                              taste—
frigid—serves his toted perfect fake member where could be love,"
    it's Manli, not so much *torpor*; misery's sum.
Don't notice, forget there, sorrow makes me look to my own dead,
    I keep no tribute from you, immured here next to nothing.
Not much writing around me now has to be copied, most
    of it at Rome—I live her Muse, love her, home, house
I lived in my best days, ill luck may hardly carp at her tastes—
    how can one small chest, I keep so little here, serve you there?
It comes to—not to live as you ask is not meant out of malice,
    did facts not rout me here, o—you know, I was generous,
what would I not risk for you—books—patiently copy out—priceless:
    all true—I 'go deferring,' copy all, seek you for it.

68a

No postmeridian ray, dear Girls, choir my Allius and *ray*,
  you wear it out—count these—you wear it—his offices—
nay if he go hence cycles, oblivion scanting his days,
  will as he woke in cold night the good deeds that stood him:
said, we come voices, voice pour out dictate all this, *this*
  multitudes affecting their like 'll chart a look at, turn a use

.... [lacuna MSS] ....

  note his cut when maggot's more to us death-cot maggots,
extend to him thence his sublimities Arachne's tale may
  desert—Allius a name her opus now foggy act.
Now, my how hermaphrodite (duplex!) Amathusia 'cured' me,
  she it is woke in me tore rue harrowed gain a re-
counting ardor wreck quantum Trinacria rubasse,
  lymph hot white like Oetea's Malia, Thermopylae's,
my saddening eyes ai see the two throb ah searing lumina flayed to
  chaos, rain trysting cheek, imbrued mothering genii.
Quelling as an aëry purl (look) gains vertical mountains—
  river's (moss) course so proves sill lit a lapping day,
quick come day prone now precipitous valley volute hues,
  pare meadow (whom?) dense see transit hither people live,
hulk of viator here, loss all in (soothe) water lave him man,
  come grave, his exhaust, who's ice to whose hellcat acres—
or quelled it as night grown jetting seas turned by night's end this
  lenient to us, aspírant aura of a second wind
and praying 'Pollux, ease, and Castor, ease, implore, ah two'—
  tally of the noblest, Allius, house islet home.
His close sown lot opened a path, it waked a 'welcome home,'
  his girl to mine—know this—his girl deeded her domain,
I'd calm common as aches her care who moves all more love.
  'Home,' my own soul, my light, candid her divine sandal—
into light of the threshold fulfilling and limning—planted—
  innocent argued a quaint sound of a sole in air;
conjugal as one time flame ran in her veins for love of
  Protesilaus Laodamia doomed home—
and kept them frustrate—no doom so sanguine when a wronged
  host of celestial gods pick at sins and curse errors.

Now in my time will me this placket, Rhamnusian virgin,
    what temerities of mine are suspect are no errors.
How jejune a pious desire of the altar for cruor—
    taste did not miss Laodamia or her hero,
could not hang on to his neck and no way there married to hold him,
    calm her veins in one or two altering winters, Hiems',
nights in bed and long as avid and saturate sweet (ah more aim)
    posset what wrapped hour tore him from her one could go on
those skimping Parcae not long to temporize 'at best' saw,
    'see my lord's marriage is set at Ilios' coast':
that time Helen aye raped, and prim horrors, Argive whoring
    (coy pair, rat) had says at Troy a care of heroes.
Troy a new fuss, common sepulchre of Asia's and Europe's quakes,
    Troy of heroes what virtue tombed, of all mankind's uncurbed
                                       sins,
and now too of our own late death, miserable my brother—
    out who lit. *Ei*, misery brother that death empties me,
ei misery brother who could not deed light to the empty,
    take him and now waste us—our tree's split, pull down the house;
o now we are taken and none part in ruin, go down as our tree,
    gone to us and with a kiss, had you lived I'd love more.
Gone on that long way, unknown interred not a soul who'll cry,
    no kinship probed no ties, compost whom no kin will raise;
sated Troy, obscene ai Troy infelicitous sepulchre
    detains in its extreme terror an alien soul o.
They'd come too proper ranks for their same old undoing poor boys,
    Greek ah pain and trials! deserted hearths' ease for cause—
'nay, Paris abductor gaffs his liberal moocher,
    o tie up a cot (two) they'll regret in time and more.'
Caught up in that cause you, pure care o my Laodamia,
    were reft too soon of his soul's kiss that queen-animate
conjugal him: taunted there absorb banes—fire, tic, air amorous,
    ice—toss in abrupt storm, day to let rot, barathrum,
gulf of errant Greek near Pheneum propped on Cyllene, one
    sucked carried emulsifying paludal soil, loam
caught, damned as once this mountain's foe ditched its medullae,
    outdid (false Zeus his parent—Amphitryon? not his)
time, bore there all care, downed Stymphalian monsters, serving a
    pure clod lord, imperious deteriorated ire—
Hercules the guileless tried thru the door of heaven and with his
    Hebe no longer virgin, hothead to forehead.

So to us all this amorous birththroe fought an ulterior low—
     quick untamed indomitable fire and you yoked to it:
nothing's that much care to a tottering grandparent, e-
     ven a happy heir his one daughter nurses, ah lit
quicks him deeding his wealth in time, invests as a witness
     'know men, attest, as entitled in these tables'—
impious derisive next of kin's goaded to other liens
     so scared that he cannot vulture! jam capital:
nothing not even o snowiest male columbine love
     comes par, how mulled too thick their improprieties,
as cool a mordant ticing pair, their care paring rostra,
     qualm, wile, pry—*keep you ay*—multivowed lost melled loves' air.
Said you wore him magnificent kissed soul of your furors,
     assembled his flavor, consoled him, gold hair, hero.
Out nil little pallor cue in time conceding her, deigned your
     looks, my ah say knows true, came to light agreed my own.
when circumstance coursing all link sigh paid Cupid o
     full gay bout crocus now candid use in tunica.
Why time *in* nets it you know one is not content Catullus,
     rare a very kind eye furthers her from us—her eye,
nay, mewing we seem a stalled whoring—mores molest her:
     sigh petty I'm—Juno mocks immaculate loving,
counting geese culpable, flagrant to conquer white ire, and
     knows, scans how many wills plural my furtive Jove is.
Ah we're devious, who means to compare the On High to us,
     .... [lacuna? mss] ....
     ingrate and trembling toll of a parent's onus.
Not that I mean he led my dear stride to duty (paternal!)
     fragrant (mm!) Assyrian vein in that odor of home—
say that furtive did it, mere ray moon who's cool a night there,
     he'd see us—*ex-hip so*, tempted, very, greet me o.
Quarry we lived satisfied, see no bee's his, doubt or unease,
     whom lapidist her love a day's candid (white) aura noted.

Here's to you—hard put to it confecting harmonious lines—
     promises, Alli, ready turns for your offices,
never strummed scabrous tang that rubbing into your name
     hide a quelling of days hiding a life hiding a life.
Who can then, deal you calm plenitude, high Themis, old hymn
     and antique solace, the moon her ray for her pious:
see this felicity, you two, smiling at you with all

304

at home whose dear love in collusion must set all homing,
would keep him our friend who noticed her arm deeded offered,
unquestioned promise, mine, of all my new time born now,
and longing into all minds, my heart, who may carry her if she
looks, my Light, quicken quivering to who'll kiss me last.

69

No lift odd mere horror, harrowed (why boy?) that no woman will,
Rufus, will yield a thigh room, suppose she sue so for more;
no selling her eye labefaction in moon ray vestees
or pellucid little delicious lapis dears.
Allied to what damn malicious fable—quote it, be fair to?
smelly soppy armpits truck so bitter a caper.
Whew can't mate a woman's—no! goat, mere fume and malice
wildest—it's
bestial! no quick-come belle lay *pugh* like cupid.
Quarry that crude loam from our noses or fumigate the pest,
ought odd mere horror design, you cur, *phew* you hint!

70

Newly say dickered my love air my own would marry me all
whom but me, none see say Jupiter if she petted.
Dickered: said my love air could be o could dickered a man too
in wind o wet rapid a scribble reported in water.

71

Securer a bo? no sacred armpits lair hops as that he-goat's—
out seeking merit with hardy podagra sick cat,
emulous he's the, tergiversator exercising your whore,
miracle cast of your nights' traumatic malignance.
Now quotidian as you to it, both tense in ulcerated ambush:
a love laid flat with his odor, himself pierced with podagra.

72

Decay bars one time, 'solely to know, see Catullus,'
  Lesbia, comparing well and then turning down Jove.
The likes of you then unknown to vulgar *as it may come*,
  so father would knot his sons, deal (league with) his sons-in-law.
Now that I've known you: quarry I'd seize impends its own fire or
  mulled in my mind it's velleity or levity.
'Keep up this zest and kiss'? Could a man timed in injuries tally,
  cog the ah marring maggots, say by now 'we love,' mean us?

73

Day, see no day—choke, qualm, quick qualm—benevolence, merit are
  out—all a whim—fear airing perhaps some few are pious.
All men are soon ungrateful, no will focuses benignant;
  the more tied to them more tired (tired) with a best of maggots:
with me here who cannot grow wise knowing nor curb his bitterness,
                                                            urged
    qualm mode o quick my one—who that quick knew the one me—
                                          gone become habit.

74

Gellius how he'd rare at pot true uncle objurgate soul array
  squeezing delicacies *they* carried out or figured.
Oke not himself a kid of writ, pot true he paired up so he'd hip some
  sure uncle-aunt: pot true had readied it, Har (poke) rot him!
Quite a will that fay kid: now qualm wise his roommate in sum
  unc' pot true *um*, where bum noway figured on pot ruse.

75

How cast down is the mind that took to my Lesbia, culprit,
  a quietus of affection, perished it heaps a soul;
what? I'm not bent to will her good to be, or see hope the mate
                                                      of eyes,
    nor desist, their ray how marring o my own, see if—who cares.

76

Seek or record then the benefactor—pree or voluptuous
    is the meaning, come say cogitate essáy pious,
no sanctum will owe loss—so feed him, not foiled there in all he
    divined not falling those numina abusing no man's,
mull to be rapt there manning a long ah high tide here, Catullus,
    sort from ingratitude good and from more a to be.
Name what, come with a man who has been, quick him, out care
                             or patience
    outfigure care, I had it, dictates—fact acquiescing;
all my honor won—ingratitude, her own credit demented.
    Why recur to the theme ample use excruciates?
Can't you animate, affirm, as what gust extinguishes, reduces
    it, this inward is—destiny's *is* is *miss her?*
Difficult best, long love submitted to no pain or ray or, more, aim.
    Difficult lest wearing out what love bid efficacies.
Your new solace high cast—who cares—the pervading kingdom:
    affect a case, see with no pity see away pity.
O dear, see me true midst misery, gods see give this one calm
    extreme moment I may see mortality lists open,
may misery as I speak of it see with time purity aching
    had ripped the hank pest and pernicious canker from me.
How may I serpents, inmost what torpor, *now* heart whose
    aches spill out, aches o my pack where were light and lightness!
No I'm not alluding one counter may yet delegate her love,
    out—cold no beauty's hest, as her poor decay will it:
in myself will a ray, hope that tight drumming deep pain purge
                             the morbid.
    O gods, ready to me all proof that my piety may.

77

Rufey my how frustrate unquickened and craved the tie I'm equal
    (frustrate? a more magnified pretty attack of malice),
sickening so breeds in me, the hot intestine hopples your burns
    ei misery surreptitious omen who knows stray boon?
surreptitious heu heu knows true cruelty and venom
    what tie, heu heu knows tried pest is of our mocked at tie.

78

Gallus ha' but brothers: bro one's lady slip's make so young she's
    all there i' this lap that feels—heir (whose) all that broth'r two
                                                                     has.
Gallus almost bellies: 'now m' dulcet young at (ah) mores,
    come pure hero with belle o belle ah pure halloa coo bed.'
Gallus ho most stilted (neck say with it) his own marriage (doom)
    keys nephew to niece—pot to remonstrate what dolt's their uncle.
Said nunc' I'd delay o, could pure ai pure ah pure girl ai
    suffer ah co-minx with spoor kiss saliva drool.
Worm with no impunity for aye, name to how many a cycle
    nose can't—wait queer, Sis Fame 'll liquidate your anus.

79

Lesbius has pooled her: kidney? whom Lesbia my—lit
    on—taking down all your gens, Catullus too ah.
Say the man who pooled her vend that combed gens of Catullus,
    see three notorieties savor or rape a rare hit.

80

Quiddity, Gelli, quarry, rosy as these too lips belie
    they burn defiant, candid hoar snow renewing
morning to homecomings, exit come too active a quiet or
    a mole longing resuscitate eighth hour of day?
'n I see o quid care taste: one very famous susurrate
    grand wee at the medial, tent a woe, horror, weary?
Sick care taste: clamant Victor his ruptured measly
    ilia, (what?) emulsion lip raw note hot (ah) serum.

81

Not many enchant you (put to it) popular is he, Juventi,
    belle who's *homo*, can't your diligence keep open your eyes
pry there qualm instead of this moribund bad seed of Pisauri
    hospice an aureate pallid decor of statue:

quitting me accord this, whom to propone and air no beast
how daze, yet no excuse cold faking us fake he is?

82

Quinti, see if't be wish of cool eyes day bear your Catullus
out all alit secret carry us best her cool eyes,
her repairing ray, no leave me those won't carry us illy
past her cool eyes seeing void carry us best her cool eyes.

83

Lesbia (my price scent t'her hero) mauls and deplores me, *'dig it'*:
he the lug fatuous Maximal Light titillates.
Mule eh nil will scent this. She knows t'obliterate would carry't,
sane is asset: now quite gone with what obloquy there,
known solely my minute, so qualms moult her cry hard to erase,
ire how tossed. I guess the hotter wit clacks with her.

84

'c-hommodating he'd bait, seeking *accommodating* willed
thicker, awed at *insidious* Arrius *hinsidious*,
at home miracle his sphere robbed a say easy locution,
come canting but a right thick's ear out *hinsidious*.
Credo (sic) *mater* (sic) Liber a one uncle of his
(sic) mater's own pa was thick sir right at cue of hi' wife.
Hoak missed so in Syria—recovering our own abused ears:
how they bind diadem high clean the air, light leave it air,
no sickly postlude of mutable hoot inhaling verbal—
comes subverting our fair turn news that is horrible, it's
Iona's flood tides, post qualm, ill look Arrius' is it?
are not *Ionia's* as he's said *Hionia's.*

85

O th'hate I move love. Quarry it fact I am, for that's so re queries.
  Nescience, say th' fiery scent I owe whets crookeder.

86

Quintia's *foremost* to multitudes; my eye can deed her *long, e-*
  rect, honest. I can go seek, single out, con, feat her
total—allow *foremost?* ah no go: nominal Venus tastes
  no life in that mighty gust, corporeal missing salts.
Lesbia's foremost, to quicken, pall care, a mate to taste,
  whom all woman as one woman's sure repute venerates.

87

No love by test, my love, 'll air then, time, say the care of all my time
  way, ray, wound time I mayed Lesbia all mate to my eyes.
No love (faith dies) allow for him whom calm furthering timed to
  continuing more to you as part there repaired to my breast.

88

Quid, fact, it is Gelli? quick'ning mother, at (queer) sis, all three
  prurient objects this spare vigil without tunics—kiss?
Quid, fog, it's his betrayed uncle no—see (nit) has he married whom?
  Eh quid squeeze quantum's ooze skippy hot, scald or hiss?
's ooze skip it, o Gelli, quantum known ultima—Tethys
  nor great Grandsire nymph Our Arm will blue it—Okeanos:
no, no ill will as quick, come scald or hiss, could prod a head ultra 's
  known see demeans so shapes to devour its glans—pity.

89

Gellius is thin why yes: kiddin'? quite a bonny mater
    tom queued veil lanced *viva*, tom queued Venus his sister
tom queued bonus pat 'truce unk,' tom queued how many plenum
                                                   pullets
    cognate is, query is his destiny *emaciate?*
Kid if he only tingled not seeing what dangler's there, honest
    can't he wish where *thin* sit maker envious.

90

Now seed their Magus (of Gelli's mother wrestling confounded
    conjunction) a son to scout as Persian haruspex in sum:
now Magus is mother knotted with son, gig nature reported,
    save verities of Persian impious religion,
now son should grow up to venerate their gods and hymns divulge
    omentum in flaming pink oil liquefyings.

91

No idea, Gelli, spurred me to mirror you faithful
    in misery! her night's trust, hope for you *more out* a foray,
quote to cognizance 'by now *constant* may waive part of him
    out posing turpitude meant to bear its opprobrium'—
saw neither your mother nor next germane (sister) would abound,
    how could she—to you—whose maimed great use ebbed in me
                                                  more.
Yet qualmish taking to your conjugal air used you
    nor saw this the cause of credo to ram assault to be.
Too sated you did see: tantamount to gaud of overweening
    gall, passing what cunning quest all wicked, 's hell, here is!

92

Lesbia may dicker simper maul or nag talk at whom, come
    dear me: Lesbia my despair ay my uneasy mate.
Question no? key the same total damn my heart: deprecate her love
    acid a way very despair I'm her uneasy love.

93

    Nil, not my aim to study you, Caesar, to be—well, a placater,
        nor score your triumph sees always another *homo*.

94

    Meantool amuck with her. Muck with her mean tool ah? Geared I
        guess to quote the cook, if she'll oil a herb bowl 'll like it.

95

Zmyrna, my own Cinna, nine harvests passed making his hymn,
    calm coped taste, Nine harvesting, edited post wintering,
meanwhile there came out in one year king gander Hortensius you
                                            know
.... [lacuna MSS] ....
Zmyrna far as Satrachi pen it who's mid depth there the wonders,
    Zmyrna can a day or cycle bear all you intend.
But Volusius' *Annals*, Padua more adventurous out fishing
    mackerel, 'll skim rip its pages wrapping a catch.
Purvey me my intimate's core, dear monument's all that there is,
    let th' populace (tumid or gaudy) eat Antimacho.

96

    See quick calm moot as gratifying the tombed—sepulchres
        how cold a ray ah knows true, Calve, dolor ay at best,
    quivers of desires and of tears that renew us our mortal loves
        all the old time amiss as flame hews, mixes with the tears,

care takes no time to move immaterial dolors of
     Quintilia, gone her young death in your immortal love.

97

No it would not mean a damn (quick whim referred to pure
                    thought) if
     thru mouth, not his end, cool my olfactory smelled Aemilio.
Now who'll moon in its soak, (no) look weigh moon his end is less
                    lewd,
     weigh room at a ham, (cool) hole's moonier and mellower:
no cincture dentures' possessed: horse dentures sesquipédal lees,
     gingivals' wear o plug ox knee ha but wetter is,
pried there a rickety palate diffuses in haste to
     empty its mule high cunny's burrow summer hot.
He figs his multitudes, he'd say fog it I see Venus home,
     yet no gristmill (no) trod it to what (quail) ass ah no?
Women seek that thing what, none will possess him but she must
     aye grow to coo loom link gear rear fate carnal figs?

98

In the, same in (when qualm?) thick wee poetry, putrid Victi,
     we'd quote—verbose as thicker whore with fatuous.
It's that coom lingua see who says *vendible*, to be possessed
     cool as it crept at us licking the carpet: an ass.
Seen as ominous wish all man's perjured there, Victi—
     hiss crass: all men 'know' (quote) cupid's efficacies.

99

Surreptitious you at bay doom loot is, my little Juventi,
     salve weigh o loom t'who'll key the whole kiss ambrosia.
Whereon with no impunity live: now my curst amplest hour
     so fixed in my summit my memory essay crooked,
doom to be may poor go neck possum flayed to abuse a least
     attempt lure as try deem more of your savage eye?

Numbed smile with the fact—'must,' mulled these diluted lips a lie
      gutters abstersive insistent finger articulates,
nay quick qualm knows thru contract mouth may not exonerate,
      taint qualm commix tie ex-whore as saliva lupus.
Pride tearing at infested misery may trade our ray Amor and
      no case quash the omniscient excruciate horror mud o,
with me ex ambrosia mutation I'm for it a lewd
      salve weigh tryst tear kiss tryst tears' hellebore o.
Why I'm cornered and poignant misery proposing no more a
      new qualm and posthaste past a kiss so ripped thru him.

100

Caelius Aufilenus' mate, Quintius Aufilena's *am*
      flow'rs Verona's 'n sum they pair and hunt (you venom)
"he" 'll frat him, *he*'ll lace her or hum. 'Who quest,' quoth thick with
                                                      ore, 'a lewd
      frater new way re th'whole cuss't sodality mm.'
Who we favor—whom—put to us? Caeli, *tibby:* now to your (know
                                                      bees?)
      perspective egregious "best" unique ah me kitty ah,
come wasting on my eyes t'her reared at flame my medulla's.
      Seize fay licks, Caeli, see as *in* and more potence.

101

Mulled hosts their countries yet mulled there by a core of wake tossed
      I've ventured these miseries, brother, our death offerings,
with the past stray more to honor my renewed remorse
      that mute and unquickened hollow queried urn, my own:
wandering when fortune ah me hid, dear, eyes you lit up—so soon,
      ah who missed her indigence brother that empty mean.
Now do mind inter here our how precious gift more our parent home
      traditional trysts tears, my renewed death offerings,
and keep here from your brother mulled many a tear he flawed to,
      of their kin perpetual, brother, ever out here fare well.

102

Secret I take it a commitment hushed to feed amica-
    bleness sealed between us *note* to feed us animate,
making us say one with those whose whole lore may adjure rite sacred,
    Corneli, the fact you may say repute me Harpocrates.

103

Out—so this means you render them, ten sestertia, Silo,
    then dare stow those qualms be savage as dumb as you choose:
out—seeing money delights don't designate quite so
    laying easy what queer and *then* savage as dumb as you choose.

104

Credit me poor to say of my life *maledictory weed die*,
    both my eyes meaning I carry her hest or curse these?
No but would I call see on myself perdition and mar her:
    cite you gone Tappo and all who make monsters their facts.

105

Meantool reconnoiters Pipléa scanning Their mountain:
    Muses fork ill ease pry kip, at him eject one.

106

Cute boy arm in elbow prize con man, kid, what do we see,
    quit credit, nor see (*say*) one there 'd rate his procurer?

107

See could we quit coveting hope taunting where hope hid and
　　　　　　　　　　　　　　　　　　　one come
　and spare want here, outcast greet you mind how appropriate.
Where I outcast greet you know peace quick me, care is your aura,
　what you restitute is Lesbia, my coveted,
restitute as coveted yet come and spare want here, herself offers to—
　know peace: o look and can day dye whiter note there!
Who is more one with felicity or what makes his hack realm
　hope taunted inviting—her care here which both there live?

108

See, Comini, popular arbitrer turned on uncanny senescence,
　spoor, cot of impurities (more abuse) to inter it,
no I cannot doubt he'd clean remove that inimical unhonored
　tongue of yours exact it avid sit it down a vulture's throat,
and force those ogle eyes worried the throats of guttural corbies,
　intestine to canines, cater to wolves membral loopings.

109

You could then, my heart, wit, eye, mean in proposing love our aim
　who knows true in turn knows perpetuating two for *our.*
Dear Mighty Ones, effect that very promise with her, posit
　and give it sink in, dear heart caught it speaks in her mouth,
to live our lot know peace, to the enduring care with time
　eternally sanctified amity of our tie.

110

Aufilena—*bonnie, simple,* laud and they're amicable:
　and keeping the pretty sum quaff a care which they institute.
To code *promised* to me a code meant to rob, 's inimical as
　code *neck tossed* 's unfair, turpitude fox foxing us.

Out of a care ingenious—is't out, no promise says *pure* decayed,
    Aufilena, would it? said dot a corrupt parry
fraud dander a fickle humus plus qualm meretricious as whoring,
    I say say total corporal prostitute.

111

Aufilena, virile content him weave her her solo,
    one partner's trust law's ay laud's! a bride's *eximious:*
said coy wish, when wish betters worse succumb where rape may rest,
    quit mothering brothers of pa's true bro your heirs.

112

Mool 'tis homos,' Naso 'n' queer take 'im mool 'tis ho most *he*
    descended: Naso, mool 'tis—is it pathic, cuss.

113

Consul (ere) Pompei O preened a duo, Cinna, so lay bound
    Maecilia: fact O' consul (ere) new kit or term
man-serve-runt duo, said craver-run t' milliform in *unum*
    singular. Fecund am semen adultery O.

114

Firmum is all too known fails so Meantool a Dives
    fare there, quite a race in say habitat *greediness,*
how coop he o many guineas, fishes, prod tract, arable, fur, ask we.
    Nay quick qualm: fruit so sumptuous eggs you per rat.
Quarry concede or sit Dives, doom of man who designed:
    salt his loud day most commodious, doom—what has he got.

317

115

Meantool inhabits in style three times ten hewed acres, forty
    quad ranging arable: count the rest in marsh sea.
Sure no the wit is with Croesus superior po't is it
    you know keen salt too t' th' mode of pose it with it,
proud turf, farmland, gentleman's silvas, cattle skew'r'd, paludal sway
    a sway out t' Hyperboreans and maritime Okeanos?
O man my god what *accent;* to men obsessed Maximus, all tare
    known *homo* said hero Meantool a man gnawn mean ax.

116

Sigh paid to be studious when I moved went on to (queer) once
    harmony, pass on to you metre of Battiades,
quit to learn then in our peace, nor could I at any rate
    tell how infested mean *your* metre ranged crushing my head,
hung wit and o me how nude frustrate *sometime* I sensed my labor,
    Gelli, neck in straits these valueless prayers.
Contra notes tell you I stay to evade you—mussed arm, sling too
    that fixes our straits, your doubts supplicate them.

Fragmenta

1. At known effigy haste my horse iambics.

2. Haunt, look you! I will dedicate consecrating Priapus,
   what home is toward Lampsacus, quag and silva, Priapus,
   Name to pray *keep you ay* in cities' hubbubs of coast lit where are
   our Hellesponti caterers oysters where sea or oar is.

3. – 0 – 0 0 day my own liquor airing libido's.

4. [0 – 0 – yet Lari o imminence Comum.]

5. Look at her what splendid summit carks her mast a moll high.

80 Flowers

[1974–1978]

to C

Heart us invisibly thyme time
round rose bud fire downland
bird tread quagmire dry gill-over-the-ground
stem-square leaves-cordate earth race horsethyme
breath neighbors a mace nays
sorrow of harness pulses pent
thus fruit pod split four
one-fourth *ripens* unwithering gaping

Starglow

Starglow dwarf china rose shrubthorn
lantern fashion-fare airing car-tire crushed
young's churning old rambler's flown
to sky cane cut back
a crown transplanted patient of
drought sun's gold firerimmed branched
greeting thyme's autumn sprig head
happier winter sculpt white rose

Mountain Laurel

Known color grown mountain laurel
broadleaf of acid earth margin
entire green winter years hoarfrost
mooned pod *honesty* open unvoiced
May-grown acute 5-petal calicoflower cluster
10-slender rods spring seed sway
trefoil birds throat *Not thyme's*
spur-flower calico clusters laurelled well

Honesty

Honesty lunar year annual anew
birdsong your lifelode blazing sunned
moon Lionmane Sickle quiet waiting
strings inner pegbox no angry
dew more alive once believed
picklock unshodding horseshoes from lofting
hooves iron zeal each lentilled
seedpod somehow mirrors luck's horseshoe

Liveforever

Wild time *liveforever* horsethyme ice
by shard green red-purple thyrse
shadowed stone or a flurry
troth *orpine* kin *acre* yellow-red
mossy stonecrop love-entangle your kind's
roof houseleek old-man-and-woman who woo
thatch song quicksilver cold would
won't know All *sedum* no

Lavender Cotton

Dwarfcypress silva evergreen spineranks branchlets
downinterlace divided leaves Great Men
sainted *rare* goldyellow globes rayless
daisies allying baskingmoth summers fragrantwool
swallows return poppyleaf grayblue white
sightwort greater-celandine to pilewort porwigle
littlefig frog buttercup arid June
rare fallen gardens *lavender cotton*

Spider or Ribbon Plant

Call exalted green leap spider
or ribbon leaf multiply rootstock
under-earth eyes buds on-earth runners
familial-lily not fathers' song   -of-the-valley
so shone argued *narcissus king's rose*
sightwort-horsethyme-spur who knows axis-white footage
spider or ribbon green housed
clustered 6-petal bells' white recurved

Sprengeri

Head a ray helix good morning
ivy red winter bronze oldest
leaves darkgreen hiddenyellow flower shypérfect
aerial rootlets shadeloving walls dark
dark contained dawns sway a
headier vine feathery sprinkling *fern-seed*
shadowed low-walls pendent family lilies
wishing you brightred berry *sprengeri*

Pussy Willow

A look at it hale
looking airs fragile bud green
looks thru catkin borne erect
bract flowers naked gold before
leaves unfold full osiers cure
headaches weaving lancets white gray
bark with thyme blown seacoast
basket the life pussy willow

Privet

League gust strum ovally folium
looped leaf nodes winter icejewel
platinum stoneseed true ebony berries
gray-jointed persistent thru green hedge
ash-or-olive order white panicles heavy
with daffodil doxy red blood pale
reign paired leaves without tooth
on edge primmed private *privet*

Charlock per Winkle

A skein bottoms them together
brassy core crux fiery yellow
fourpetal fivepetal salver blue solitary
winkle springgreen wellwintered leaves bright
trails creep white thyme times
fieldmustard with myrtle dogbane minor
quillet praises lacquer truemustard ox-beef
weeps *uncrossed charlock bluer winkle*

Heart's Ease

Heartsease heart's ease love-in-idleness viola
tricolor bluepurple white yellow hoard
tenses straggle some mule purchase
violet not gold for sounding
Ladies'-delight places gold barren
stemsquare soundpost Johnny-jump-up petalled five
four in pairs unbleeding heart aflower
the lower fifth twice-spurred nectar

Cinquefoil

Potent tiller reck to copper
silveryyellow sulphur notched hearts rose
with the wild roses field
roadside waste 5-leaflets or 7
you roughfruited 5-fanwise *cinquefoil* rival
desert-fluted rose-mauve the cardinal while
minting white-thyme assures bees roses
summersun honeyyield together rained upon

Venus's Looking-glass

Bell-looking-glass upright leaf-shells ring the
herb stem two flowers climb
come May near-ground-axil seeded unopened
clasp soon June higher perféct
red-purple specular as speculum venery's
mirror-bell flowers one for three
no harebell hanging chase *azur'd*
veins flight faced skies unseen

Spearmint

Mint a spiked attar hot
lavender spiced laundered savoury purpled
ground-covering runners lilac-brilliant flower square-rooting
stems thyme's spikes better often
replanted thoughts grown wild olive
haunt pungencies in an old
coat in us buff-green distant
cotton-glaumer smoke trees pierce *spearmint*

Zebrina etc

Trades scant aware is plentiful
the *dayflower* broken stem-bits root
bleed uncoil East is 3
petals 2 night-blue the third
white a spathe hides above
healed boat-leaves wandering worlds miscalled
creeping-charleys butt nearer a day's
red 3-petal-heart perpend *zebrina etc*

Four-o'clock

Nicked a gin-ace seeing hour
a bitter herb core horrors
poor man's weatherglass cloudburst sun
pimpernel *weed it* and funkia
plantain leaves hosting their flowers
only companion-bells each recall *no*
in galas an attic stairs
evening timeless days sun four-o'clock

Cockle

When cockle takes over it's
cowherb is rife bruised lanceleaves'
sap an airy-ah where cow-care's
sedge tail drunk o'the corn
love's snail a fort-likeness sails
seas in cockles soft horns
of 5-petal weave with 5-sepal
flower lamps white brighten pink

Petunia

What's in a name *that's*
homeborn arrowroot when arrowhead is
meant pet tune a smell
earshell wampum potato-eye dark-horse mórel
rainband petunias yearly end crimped
bosom-flounces funnelled curled quoin star-center
iceblue-flown numb you light wild
strains sun sole less woods

Wild Geranium

Not a friend hated time
must friend or end heads'
May-scent mint all poor legacies
Run-away-Robin leaf blue purpling scallops
gleek home marsh foolish-fire pennyroyal
two-lipped pudding-grass weeds dress earth
cranesbill-fruiting-beak wild geranium unhedged deepest
to uproot the reed oak

Rose-of-Sharon

Rose-of-Sharon lilac-red blown hibiscus searing
all cues of soft leaves
swamp pale lustres odor of
musk the thrown burning brand
seas glare coast-winds reel high-pitched
alterant names descrying black-hellebore white
white double-flowered *marsh-mallow mallow-rose snowstorm*
sea-hollyhock torn not thorned rose

Chrysanthemum

Marguerite-chain all color not royal-or-blue
boll samited *costmary* perennial herb
askance leaf jagged feather pinching
October *feverfew* short-rayed part then
home abreast *oxeye* yellow disk
long white doublepetal look cant
a *mum* time *goldenflower* far
East spring winter hearts renew

Bayberry

Candleberry bayberry spice resinwax green
durant leaf moor in key
dour attested deer-wit winds survive
days *hippos* rampant *wooden* ancient
standstill plummet unprotected laurel crown
trust sweet-fern of your family
bring birds alula sound coast-floes
sand-iced willows *compt* gibbous moons

White Begonia

Indoor winter white begonia fibril
creeper begun soggy stemjoint cut
2-lipped salver recalling grove wedding-basket
constant white fire falling warmth
baby's-breath gypsum-loving teas since hances
white camellia hope winter-leggy outdoor
zinnias arm perennial rays summers
white begonia suns 5-lobed indoor

African Violet

Open rosette flowering continually cyme
neither guess nor erasing eye
ion anta terminal blossom earliest
pinked-white perfect-double veined tree-of-life greenest
hair-smoothèd bare a knot planter
thrifty leaf underleaf purple grown
temperate tempered sanctum tho no
land or violet spring brings

Coleus

Coleus *foliage plant* coleus bloom
eyed-leaf fare soft velvet indoors
winter north vair toothèd frills
greenedged red-spotted or-   leafstalk pink-cream
midwest *java* fact the old-world
insheathed tropic shoottips spared frost
summer outdoors blue mint-lilac raceme
richer leaf *The* Foliage Plant

Tulip

Blizzard sun upturn tulips chances
bare earth guess near in
honor breed true as the
lilies wakerobin naked bulb turban
wejack shadow *early* crocus iris
thinnest leafblade many seed air-thread
still livid tulip to leaf
green blue pointed heart valentines

Crocus

Hear it tease question will
the snowdrop come up nodding
green in white crome asea
navvies long a crook tip
strung alack riches look o
into scaleless bulbs a false
spring snowpits measure hours sative
crocus furnace sandy yellows cloth-of-gold

Forsythia

Forced yellow spring before crenated
green unfolding fortune eye holly-
ember firethorn winter low stonecrop
thyme bluewinkle lilac forsythia suspense-arched
glance 4-petal goldenbell closer strapped
vine pith stem arch aged
branches root their height steep
smoke breathe olive branch dove

^

Pachysandra

Naked spike chocolaty men white
lances girl sewing-awl down stem
flowers join over evergreen saw-edge
upsúrge pack in sandy rows
cover ground sun shade the
term it all is box-leaf
winterer white blossom East spurge
when *spring beauty* goes quicked

Violet

Viol lace each stilled note
color two-petal pairs out of
five one heart cup yearly
white violet-streaks leave pointed-scoop
greener other more a round
purple gold centers down white
tree shadow if no rose
too near to be bruised

Deutzia

Lotus of toy china bells
numerous pent amorous white blossoms
recurved gracile japanned gray yellow
stems dewed see your oblong
bluish leaves green cities sacks
if rage scent drugged roadsides
lotus fruit spin oaths a
night amulet hardby white deutzia

Lilac

Sere ring a pipe wood
lodging sweet by tempest lodged
nose knows two colors pale
and deep lilac blossom breezed
pruned some red fall-scattered bloom
hesperis purple mother-of-evening gone spring
angels in bustles deep lilac
pales lilac angels for white

Azalea

Foul weather sighs old time
may is so unfurnished walls
drown tears azalea wills barrens
dry long heath be friend
south lion's-ear tale red north
chalices leaf winter greener wet
azalea longs no dry death
climbs crimson treading roman shades

Lily-of-the-Valley

At low cost woodlands con
veil area may a lease
brought home revive next may
carpeting leaf veins crossings sunned
languish dawns yellowrocket petal-cross sundown's
incense close companion late chains
shade one-side clasp angled scapes
mog white little bells valley

Grassflower

Clay tone your purple arrives
from deep tubers pussley partially
kin touched wilt *spring beauty*
good-morning-spring weed salvage moist-eyed daystar
obscures married eras integrity lost
spoor midsummer forest returning *mayflower*
lanceleaves shield buds kinless royal
gold-glint eyed purple silkiest throat

Clover

Clover nitrogen soak airily pumps
phosphor dark shiner niter direland
forage 4–5-6 rarely more leaflets
shamrock doublin' confusion red globe
blossom trifling home prate tense
dutchwhite repents yellow's *nonesuch* black
medic disputes none 's shamrock
perennial springers onto bog falls

Roses

Roses hardy as clover return
the wild no quirk-thorobred notched
5-petal evening-shining knit to the
pasture valley-scent *old teas damask*
pink *sweetbrier eglantine* white today
miniatures floribunda grandiflora tho new
restore purple-rose *Angel Face Handel* white
figures redoubled *climber* pink-edging invests

Phlox

Flux ablaze flog a new
wine look now's fast lamp-lighting
corymb high poop of ships
fires ring rose blood ruby
branching raise round ladders leaves
clasp full flame in sight
valerian purple papule *wild sweet*
william jack-pudding trumpets *jacob's ladder charity*

Dutch White Iris

Irides swordblade road *dutch purple*
grassleaf wilt *blue-eyed grass* turned
violet rinks kneeing grassleaves curvet
mementos dutch white iris return
see how dear apricot-yellow touch
grows april white 3-outer narrow
fiddle-waist *falls* 3-inner smaller *standards*
all told six based with *hafts*

Snowflake

Wanting throat crown narcissus proves
snowflake essáy a pace so cloud
pool ignorance spring surprise
in vent toss wit a white-green
6-star-widened nodding flowerfoot papersheath'd
leaf rapier next greater celandine
cobweb-kell 'd own May's snowflake
white yellow stacked glimpse shut

Honeysuckle

Honeysuckle loner serry rampant zone
locust dry wire half-evergreen hang
in sky sigh loss t'whom
May wood or bone sigh
clew men 'n' flourish in rubbish
caper 's sunless flowers upper-lip 4-lobe
lower- born leaf-axil 5-white yellowfading
adam's natural birds twig-'n'-berries comprehend

Marigold

Marigold keep the dogs away
witjar knot ill-lustrious kale canned
thus no thrust kin godhead
nurley scented leaves faint-teeth warn
day rayflower nightclosing th'gates path
you lack chair-days shadow-marshes *kingcup*
cowslip May-blob gools recalled *marsh-marigold*
no lost happiness lives healed

Lilies

Called *Niobe* high more callous
gnar's th'sum talk's shrill pine
bog-asphodel echo echo serious
light *jacob's rod* sceptre go on
so made of days lilies
do not mourn orange-yellow lilac-blue-white
pleached meek stone deepened asphodel
anthers' coast tallest of all

Queen Anne's Lace

Top-turfy gimp fiery oes eyes
light white flat lacy heads
centrums purple many uneven small
flowers each whorl umbel if
awry ladies songflawed wit pretty 's
well queen unwanted princess throws
horse prize wild carrot autumn
hurdle stands jackdaw-course carried her

Chicory

Seacorps hint imbues blues *blue*
sailors blueweed blue dandelion monksbeard
low backward-bent leaves outdo lettuce
thinned bluetooth'd rays impassioned keek
core and mires steed *coffeeweed*
chicóryĕ succory 's bitter tea 's palaver
horse-seas bow kiss fill'em on
concur it ur hoar-eye memento

Dandelion

No blanch witloof handbound dry
heart to racks a comb
lion's-teeth thistlehead *golden-hair earth nail*
flower-clock *up-by-pace* dandle lion won't
dwarf lamb closes night season
its long year *dumble-dor* bumbles
cure wine *blowball* black fall's-berry
madding sun mixen seeded rebus

Dahlia

Interest grows not knowing dahlia
what color blossoms dividing tubers
eyes upward toward old stems
assure curled in white-tipped purple
moonrays or all-white glass-mask disks
roses cannot excel you thornless
pleasing comeling birds black-eyed susan
dahlia year's-heads income the same

Impatiens

Impatiens impatience luckless wit *touch-me-not*
clouded deplore each other fool
instant blues hushed seed *jewelweed*
balsam-mean aspires hell's-sidewalk flowers leaflance
allayed rarest star kiss young
old-rose purple white also heart-leaf
garden balsam whole stay indoors
scarlet-tuned slender-spur outdoor evenings summer

Slipperwort

Spirit of quickness reading *slipperwort*
paradise garden no familiar softening
ponderably light unresonant turf olive
windsown moss north's unhoused *calceolaria*
crenated yellow-spotted orange-brown 2-lipped
slippers upper smaller book south-kissed
with its kin escape paulownia
compassion reifying whirring thought hardy

Chokecherry

Prune us serried teen sear
ease autumn *wild black cherry*
old pod-husk fence birds stock
clouds white aster-rays spinet-locust white
roses' kind late-ripe dint-incurved leaves
cicala leap 's *go-go-go* early waking
early-evening *can-can-can* distance cricket mutes
squirrel mouth-dart spread twig twigs

Snowdrop

Snow names a wreath *snowdrop*
2-year-sleep look-on tie bulb Oh
say earthleaf lagnappe midwinter huddle
futural *snowflake* aft *snowdrift* sweet
alisoun not madness kneevalleys harp
snowtrillium woodland dwarf-white *snowpoppy east*
moss starry chickweed *snow-in-summer snow-on-the-mountain*
snowberry bears white-fruit *snow-wreath* nine

Snow-Wreath

From solitary flowerstalk some fingers
fragrance look down ridge-back enamel
leaves *snowdrop* impetal seagreen unseen
months *snowflake* unplanted *snowdrift* sweet
alyssum self-risen *snowtrillium* new valleys
east *snowpoppy snow-in-summer* starry grasswort
prairie *snow-on-the-mountain* wilding seacoast
snowberry-drupe snow-wreath earth-rounds bees' rose

Grecian Windflower

Peer re foot own his
story as no grecian or
anemone *dutch bulb* starves promises
die anthers carry off fill
us sparse scent choose which
true name red-pink-purple rays yellowed
green discs keen ens seas
betrayed sold neglected ponent anemone

Windflower

Windflower overworld selvageflame sun coddle
lay dune ass toss opt
thrown own candle urge shade
unhated unloved unseen slight bud
windflower singled erst field-lily nods
unshaded whorled th'solitary flower suns
clouds summers asleep crowfoots spring-*rue*
anemone leaves flowers both earth

Grape-Hyacinth

Where wildered anemones hay-lei moony
'*a-dutch-treat*' fingerhigh nightblue spring's last
grape-hyacinth sations wilt minúte turned-down
urns segment dense perianths pale-teeth
musk harries raceme owes scented
plum earth-channelled leaves *wild hyacinth*
squill reads no script *hyacinth-throes*
name *love-in-absence regret* to regret

Hyacinth

Who hock in toss regret
regret Ai-hyacinthus veined petal eyes
point to *larkspur* summers spring-*amaryllis*
pale-teeth perianth limb *spart* rue
dens earth's-floor abundance *iris* spire
rows *gone-back* small stalks under
earth swords nodes knot *gladíolus*
calm *gladden gladwyn gladwin glad*

Dogwood

Coo-saw kin-ens sees seas season
daw-gunned earth night planet *cornel*
home forced people ember-eves ember-days
sanguine horn skewerwood midnight sun
temperate mayjune empery *bush bunchberry*
highforest subtly flowered notched-bracts red
white pink impetal fruit blues-white-red-orange-black
crown *one*-spring coldspell *dogwood-winter snowball*

Poppy Anemone

Poppy anemone chorine airy any
moan knee thinkglimpsing night wake
to short-wages no papàver world-wars
opiate bloodroot puccoon indian-dyed fragile
solitary gloss-sea powderhorn yellow-orange West
earthquake-state sun-yellow tall-khan *poppy corona*
airier composite eyelidless *bride bridge*
it uncrowned birdfoot spurs *dayseye*

Spirea

Meadowsweet centuries friends allowably carol
lineal plinius names *spiry* thicket
old house-sites haul thick-ey'd horse
toméntose no-sting no honey mopus
sun-steed water unbridled harangue maybe
argued can nod dew day
hardhack steeplebush roseate or standing
smoke white thrive bridal wreath

Narcissus

On no mat appear echoer
paperwhite waterfull lorn knar kisses
wilderness rock mother *Sleyd-silk* climing
sorrow Elements below voice cuckoo-brake
scaped taciturn shade strumpet hose-in-hose
yellow joss-flower iris-rapiers *pheasant's eye*
chime-red-crown spread limb whitest solitary
sun-roundelays paper-thin throat poet *narcissus*

Bearded Iris

Gay ore geek con candlelows
driveway west fanswordleaves equitant stride
meteor aery creamwhite *falls bearded*
pard-yellow spotted *standards* gules bees
knuck to min hours crewroar
thyme our booty us east
bluepurple lapilli broad weigh Libra
short month candelabrum amaryllis paper

Lily-of-the-Valley Fortunei

Fortunate sheer a mile's upmost
round how well-leaved flowered impórtun'd
not white th'pink rare *fortunei*
a *lily-of-the-valley's* her family *true*
solomon's seal May mutant earthstemmed
lean-tos asides color cite Whose
corms lie low rise *false-spikenard*
leaves zigzag avail dark-hues plant

345

Oxalis

Wood-sorrel lady's-sorrel 3-hearts tow ox
a leese rapids whose soul
air-spring disperses thru water elator
ox lips mistaken for clover
more ruse mulberry locust-flower shield
welcome wanderer *óxalis* time primrose-yellow
a breeze sweet rampant pulse
scald scold honor the bard

Alpine Rosy Bells

Hillocky *alpine rosy bells* name
mountains earth heaps bulbs flowering
first bud brown turn rosy
upturned limbed cups pygmies silvery
anthers black to clouds dutch-art
amiss aspire least pink lightpierced
papery barber poles vanish discords
swallows uptrilled-thundershower horses slope from

Jade

Stemclasp becomes two *cross you*
lar again tier on tier
africa shore stable arms spiraling
stonecrop weathervane *bay laurel's noblest*
forest-cluster open small white
centered-yellow thick leaves olive green
frost free desert guerdon smaller
houseplant unfleshly years return stemclasp

Artemisia

Art to me's hear stellary
honor never translated my sum
pauper in aerie white *dusty-miller*
feltsmooth *lad's love* disc-buttons dull gold
neume nod grace discord concord
a breath *beach-wormwood suthern wude*
brush cottony *sightwort* booklice blur
old eyes-iris evergreen retainers sun

Wild Honeysuckle

Wild honeysuckle minim *azalea* nude
to flora honey bees visit
for combs believed poisonous naked
miniature magenta sconce bud open
five-petal limbed earthward taper light
taper-wise peri climb many days
paradise dim covert yellow heath
alight soundless gently renewing fall

Telephus Sedum

Tell of us sedum comic
course a zone *everlasting* fuses
hue green questions cosmos nods
tell of him sempiternal octobers
seat white-purpling house-roof *hen-'n'-chicks* or
no anthers a kor homer
grass-widow's *goldenmoss* weigh little lovely
rosette-climbing-3's two-lip dropper bred true

Yarrow

Bottoms *milfoil yarrow* holm seas
herb-ah-dand *turkey hen* leg it
toles odd astral eaves rust
sticks urban miraculous ditty whinnied
to few gains coastfoamed mares
unharrowed *ptarmica* fern-daisy centers few
rays grace forest charms arch
chill ear knows weathers flame

Butter-and-Eggs

Ranstead yellow fringes dragon clusters
umbrella-leaf lin airy a wool
gare as *snapdragon* snatched fruit
burning brandy under the Dragon's
tail of fool's-fame paint thought
slumber dial's point near enough
sooner than glory beyond hearts
butter-and-eggs snow down the slide

Aster

A star tow ash stow
rote crowd mickle mass *daisy*
frostflower lazytongs lightning *aster* risk
your fire anneal generous gentle
baited shadow some moss-burn'd summer
evergreen-winter connect a cut clay
aurous quick gnomon he'll mellow
lucre head purple black study

Raspberry

Thimbleberry redcap odor art whose
cow'd thorn-pang'd hammer-finger unhooks palmate
fill loss-afar empty-cup eaten wild-native
rose-flower'd mated with other brambles
seeded-pulp dewberry plethoric blackberry drunk-red
boysenberry loganberries *phenomenal* such-of-you tastier
scent a rick case global-peat-cranberry
whortleberry twain huckleberry flatulence th'*raspberry*

Daisy

Bellis perennis daisy of history
ing lace water-formed a hid
pin-eyed thrum-eyed brehon-rule eve adam
adam eve meadows birth-hymn drupe-studded
strawberry oversell spring-freeze whipperwill storm
pied-daisy rays vogue green-erin discs
may not excel white double-ray largess
sails-gold-discs heritage *fort at Montauk*

Aloe

Álow álow loo no words
Oliver-error Rowland to Tower came
eyebright monkeyshines monkey-wrench whitespotted eyetooth
Adder's-tongue juice 'll streak kill-courtesy
mule-bitter-aloes fancies of boor succulence
Bermoothes thrust rapier's-point barb Ā-doze
stemless-lilies-internode more a lów E
mellows habit swept dust or

Thyme

Takes time where wild the
thyme blows poor tom's a
cold relentless-vest muffler jacket coat
one bluegreen eye ate his
hope sevenyear fanned eyesack disrailing
birds'-tread hie *rose* tree-budding fire
moon's flight twice sun's spider-manor-borne
litter letter words-justice *thyme* righting

Vines

You vines wreathe sands printless
coil *bittersweet waxwork* most bound
free walls fall-arils scan dense
mushrooms gathered gentler than *grapevine*
columned pied *clematis* life's white
withywind *wistaria* nods *traveler's joy*
magenta-climb 3-bract *bougainvillea* seafroth floret
nasturtium-leaf what most it heart

Weeds

Founderous wilding weeds endear paradise
smallhead *bluecurls* blue-wool'd *romero* defer-ah
bamboo-suh *downyrattlesnake* pact is pubescence
feed talk bananas great maulin'
favor'd *henbit chara* no wars
goldenrod solid-day go ponder otter
blue-boneset scut-redshank *ladysthumb* smilax *herb-patience*
ascending *tansy field-bindweed lady's-orchid-slipper* foison

"X"

Of thousands grown climb head-on-head
A "X" unknown stand indued
no glue kiss'd peon knee
freesia's iris grass-tropical true scourge
bees earthflight magnetic north 4-native
dial-canter excellence scent one-thousandth-in
one-night *lady's-eardrops-fuchsia* seaborne northeast unnailed
papyrus-bath-nut *trailing arbutus fringed-gentian hydrangea*

Yaupon

Children nurs'd woods tilled rock
red totem dances blacks drink
under eyes threshold index thunder
Yaupon flower-scurried buds eyes glance
magnified throb aye lex foam't
horse a full bolus leaf-wave-edged
evergreen prove if berries hardy-bred
'junivals' gulp'm tiger-numb current-red

Zinnia

With prayer-plant eyes annually winter-leggy
zinnia miracles itself perennial return
blest interim strength lengthening coreopsis'-summers
actual some time whereso near
zebra-fragrant sharpened wave currents tide
new moon to full sunrise
sunset enable ships seaworth slow-rounds
rosette lancers speared-yucca's white night

Gamut
[1978]

Gamut

Much ado about trees lichen
hugs alga and fungus live
off each other hoe does
dear owe dear earth terrace
money sunday coffee poorjoe snow

Index of First Lines and Titles

Titles of poems are printed in **boldface** and *italic boldface*. First lines of poems are printed in roman and *italic*.

357